Springs
of Life
in the Spirit

Bishop Rodrigo Romano

Published by Ibukku
www.ibukku.com
Graphic Design: Índigo Estudio Gráfico
Copyright © 2020 Bishop Rodrigo Romano
ISBN Paperback: 978-1-64086-893-9
ISBN eBook: 978-1-64086-894-6

Índice

Introduction

*"Let us draw near with a true heart, in full assurance of faith, having
our hearts sprinkled clean from a guilty conscience and our bodies washed
with pure water."* Hebrews 10:22.

**"*L*et us therefore, surrounded as we are by a cloud of testimony, cast out all
the sin that besets us. Let us run with perseverance to the battle appointed
for us, looking unto the high and consummate of faith, Jesus Christ, the Lord of
lords, the King of kings in view of the joy that was set before him, who endured the
cross without ignomiy, and by his grace is seated to the right hand of the throne
of the Father" (Hebrews 12).**

As we begin this spiritual work, above all, our goal is to bring our human nature
as close as possible to the supernatural power of the Blessed Trinity. Christ is eternally our ideal of perfection and we are invited to grow to his stature, *"...until we
all attain to the unity of the faith and of the knowledge of the Son of God, to a
perfect man, to the measure of the stature of the fullness of Christ; that we may no
longer be children, tossed back and forth and carried about with every wind of
doctrine, by the trickery of men, who deceive by the cunning craftiness of deceit;
but speaking the truth in love, may grow up in all things into him who is the lead,
even Christ..."* (Hebrews 4:13). In the best moments of life, when we find ourselves
inspired to live the abundance of grace and deeds, loving all, cherishing all, always
seeking the good in everything, we cannot find a better example of what intimate
communion with Christ means, that is, the stripping away of our own interests in
order to unite ourselves fully, the grace of a relationship of true communion. The
worthiest men of all ages, the patriarchs, the kings, the prophets, the apostles, the
martyrs, the saints, true witnesses and champions of the faith, all these could only
excel in attaining the brightness of God's unfading glory through the attainment of
the primary goal of the tireless pursuit of communion.

Christ incarnate reveals to humanity the human face of the Father and the eternal and infinite capacity of God to reach down into the inmost depths of creation
in order to rescue and restore supernatural dignity in Christ. *"All of you who were
baptized in Christ are endued with Christ."* (Galatians 3:27). *"Him who, being
in the form of God, did not regard equality with God a thing to be grasped, but*

emptied himself, taking the form of a servant, being made in the likeness of men; and being found in appearance as a man, he abased thyself, becoming obedient to the point of death, even death on a cross." **(Philippians 2:6-8).**

Just as the rainbow exhibits in its power the softness of the different colors and enchants from the smallest to the largest eyes, because its beauty is in the reflection that exalts the sun's rays, so every human being in fullness of dignity is invited by the grace of God to make of his body and soul an exultant plasma capable of reflecting the powerful rays of the spiritual beauty of Christ. This invites us to take a definitive step towards the discovery of new realities, to be part of the discovery of the new power that exists within each being, that only by grace, can be touched from the personal desire for change and self-improvement towards the most excellent.

You may ask yourself then: How to reach this level once the mind and heart are so scattered and our life is so full of hurry, tiredness, fatigue, oppressions, fears, illnesses and disturbances? **In truth, the answer is not as complex as the question is simple, to imitate Christ is to assume exactly the commitment to follow his teachings.** The path begins with wanting with all thought and disposition of inner strength provided, to begin a process of unblocking the mind and all the prejudices that one has to approach a full truth exceeding in all the truth that has led him throughout life. I am convinced that for many people life has not been easy, especially because they have had to fend for themselves and now, discovering Christ so powerful, so supplying, so generous, so caring, causes us to be frightened and afraid to let go completely. Such an amazing experience and discovery **is like the man who, after climbing to the top of the mountain, realizes that after overcoming all the obstacles of the climb, it is difficult and almost impossible to jump into the void.**

Knowing Christ moves us to a challenge to jump, not to emptiness, but to the overflowing fullness that will lead us to empty ourselves to then begin a new fullness that exceeds our desires, our will, our personal covenants and our objectives; our fears and uncertainties, our own expectations, while climbing that mountain. Imagine yourself with a glass full of dirt and filth between your hands, it is inevitable the desire to clean it because it is in our nature, to seek cleanliness, conformity, the pleasing aesthetics of satisfaction, even if it is not in the general levels and patterns. I might say that even the person who lives in the greatest disorder, accumulating things, seeks in this state of disarrangement its point of adjustment and order in the disorder. To submit to Christ means to let all that is impure be undone by the touch of what is purest by the intervention of God's grace, **no one can change unless he is definitely determined to receive the stroke of the Holy Spirit.** It is true and certain that by ourselves we cannot, we are trapped by a filth that comes from sin itself which originally settled upon our very existence and thus dominated us by putting us under the yoke of Satan himself. *"Therefore, as by one man sin entered into the world, and death by sin, and so death spread to all men, because all sinned."* (Romans 5:12).

I. Following Christ

"Be imitators of God, therefore, as well-loved children" Ephesians 5:11.

"But we all, with unveiled face, beholding as in a glass the glory of the Lord, are being transformed into the same image from glory to glory, as by the Lord, the Spirit." 2 Corinthians 3:18.

The imitation of Christ reflected in Jesus' 40-day fast in the desert directly teaches us that the fast was not only a victory over the human body of Jesus, but rather, it was a supernatural victory capable of being reflected in Christ's battle against the wiles, deceptions and enchantments of Satan. ***"Then Jesus was led up by the Spirit into the desert, to be tempted by the devil. And when he had fasted forty days and forty nights, he was hungry, and the tempter came to him, and said unto him, If thou be the Son of God, command that these stones become bread. And he answered and said, It is written, Man shall not live by bread alone, but by every word that proceedeth out of the mouth of God. Then the devil took him into the holy city, and set him on the pinnacle of the temple, and said unto him: If thou be the Son of God, cast thyself down: for it is written, He shall give his angels charge over thee, and in their hands they shall bear thee up, lest thou dash thy foot against a stone. Jesus said unto him, It is written also, Thou shalt not tempt the Lord thy God. Again the devil took him up into a very high mountain and showed him all the kingdoms of the world and the glory of them, and said to him: All these things I will give you if you will fall down and worship me. And Jesus said unto him, Begone, Satan: for it is written, Thou shalt worship the Lord thy God, and him only shalt thou serve. Then the devil left him, and behold, angels came and ministered to him."*** **(Matthew 4:1-11).**

The human being with integrity who wants to follow Christ cannot skimp on the commitment to battle and the effective right to victory. Following Christ means just realizing the intention of Satan's attacks and his cunning ways of subjecting us to ignominy and denial of spiritual values, because those who follow Christ will constantly be subject to Satan confronting us and trying to take us by the force of his deceptions. The following of Christ leads us by faith to the able, faithful and true victory against all the snares, entanglements and evil machinations of this infernal spirit of division, which aims to destroy the children of God. ***You really can be*** *happy and happiness begins with the realization that you can, that you do have within you an inexorable force that calls you to be a better person, especially now that you can understand the power of love within yourself. This is the experience after the catharsis, which is to empty oneself to the innermost depths and to fill oneself little by little, reaching autonomy, freedom and happiness in faith.* Only those can be happy who live this process consecutively, but also gradually, at mature levels, without a single instant ceasing to be carried out this same process in a concrete and real way.

If you want to follow Christ you must embrace obedience as your inner teacher, only it can teach you the serene sense of loving submission and the desire to listen to the teaching that comes from the mouth of God in a humble way, capable of leading you to responsible maturity in his deeds, thoughts and perceptions. Jesus, to the Pharisees, always said: *"He who sees me sees the Father, he who hears me hears the Father; no one can come to the Father except through me, I am the way, the truth and the life"* (**John 14:6**). For a person who wants to be happy and understands that there is no happiness without intelligence, he observes the strict importance of being obedient. **Healed intelligence, educated and directed towards God, makes us rest in the wisdom that comes from the high heavens, obviously this same intelligence enlightened by wisdom, will lead us docilely into the arms of obedience of faith.** To be obedient does not mean to be a person imposed to an ignorant, immature and blind submission. Obedience, when it is established by faith in the mind of the one who wishes to follow Christ, reveals greatly the character of the free and enlightened person, who assumes to obey and listen with docility, calmness and grace, the soft voice that comes from God. **So, if God speaks to me and I can listen to Him, it is a clear sign that He, in His power, is with me and I with God. How can I make mistakes?** Mistakes are exactly what make us unhappy, so we can say that the only way to happiness is solid, mature, humble and simple obedience to the imitation of Christ. **The process of listening not only fills up our space of relationship with God, but definitely expands our maturity and unmistakable capacity for building new relationships nourished by the light of true joy that we have received in Christ Jesus.**

Christ, gentle and obedient unto death and death on a cross. Can you imagine what mature obedience meant for Christ? Being God, he did not spare the grace reserved for him, but lowered himself in profound obedience to the mystery of God in order to save and engender in all humanity the eternal possibility of the full and effective rescue of created nature, making it new through the mystery of the cross, through his wounds, through the shedding of his most precious blood, through his loving passion, through his forgiveness of reconciliation; He brought us out of the captivity of darkness and rebellion to make us capable of being introduced into the

New Covenant in order to definitively assume the new condition of heirs. This is called salvation.

If you really want to live this obedient happiness following Christ, you need to learn something very big that you will have to carry with you all your life. I speak directly of the spirit of renunciation, of the ability to, in an intelligent way, reject what does not serve you, the poor and childish, weak and wrong preferences of a life led by pleasures and disobedience, to begin now, little by little, to learn to make new choices, to make new and forceful decisions, to give yourself the opportunity to evaluate all the stretches of personal history with the desire to make new arrangements and repairs. *As Jesus taught us, we cannot follow two masters, we cannot submit to two laws, we cannot mix night and day.*

Every space of our existence, every step, every sense that we perceive or feel, every apprehension, every discovery along this process, at the same time that it touches us, provokes us and the sense of our being is not in the symptoms of the provocations but in the consequences of the actions from our choices; whoever knows how to be provoked and is able to discern the provocation of the light of obedience to the following of Christ, for sure will know in the end to make the best choice, not to lose but to win, and win in Jesus Christ.

"We also know that God disposes all things for the good of those who love him, whom he has chosen and called. Those whom he foreknew he also predestined to be like his Son and to be like him, that he might be the firstborn among many brethren. Therefore those whom he chose, he called; those whom he called, he made righteous and holy; to those whom he made righteous and holy, he gives glory". (Romans 8:28-30).

II. Resignation, the way to faith

"If any man would come after me, let him deny himself, and take up his cross daily, and follow me". (Luke 9:23).

If you want to follow Christ, you must understand that resignation is not an option towards misery, dissatisfaction or towards the worst. If at first resignation seems to you a loss, an act of abandonment to uncertainty, ***once you have examined the demands contained in the process of resignation and once it is put into action, experienced, felt and overcome, it will give you strength, autonomy, freedom and happiness in Christ Jesus. The process of resignation is one of the most touching in our entire life, because to renounce is a task for the brave, the strong and those who are able to reinvent and recreate starting from scratch. Resignation is the change of vision, of terrain, of plans, of friendships, of focuses, which before were very important, but now, in the light of new life, we are able to understand that some things have lost and must lose their protagonism so that the new life leads us essentially to true human and spiritual growth.***

Throughout my priestly ministry I have met countless people with a deep desire to be united to Christ. They are wonderful people, sweet, kind, loving, beloved, very intelligent, great professionals, people who even had victories in their lives, but still unable to renounce in fullness. I would like to warn that there is no such thing as partial resignation, we cannot renounce 50%, exactly half, **the resignation has to be total and it involves your three levels of existence, the dimension of the body and all its desires, of the soul and all its longings, of the spirit and all its invocations, this is called resignation for conversion.** Following Christ is truly a process of **"metanoia"**, which means transformation. The Apostle Paul knew how to translate into words exactly the essence of his experience and intimacy with Christ: ***"It is no longer I who lives, but Christ who lives in me"*** **(Galatians 2:20).**

For a path so exuberant with so many challenges that is the following of Christ, every man, every woman, every integral human being, needs nourishment, proper provisions for the spiritual life. The aspect of spiritual nourishment was, during all these centuries, essential matter of the discussion around the faith, ***the entire Bible, the revealed word of God, is a magnificent banquet for the essential nourishment of the people of God.*** However, to enjoy this nourishment, still for the vast majority of people is to approach an unknown field that many of us are still afraid and uncertain of how to start, where to start and why start. **Despite the need for God, we are afraid to approach this fountain of knowledge**, this flowing spring of divine delights, revealing mystery of tradition and grace, supplementing our intimacy with God. *It is compared to the child who anxiously awaits the summer to be able to go with his parents to the river and enjoys every moment of the trip and longs for the camp, however, when he peeks at the river bank, enchanted by its beauty, depth and power, he is prevented from diving in and enjoying the river, preferring to continue his vacations playing only on the bank just throwing pebbles. He spends all his time watching the waters move, but without giving himself the opportunity to move in them.*

It is fear that prevents us from learning, it is complexes, prejudices, traumas, wounds and incorrect longings that do not allow us to focus on the main objective of our existence: **to know God, to love him above all things and to live the abundance of his love.**

If you want to follow Christ you must learn that if you go to the river, it is to get wet and live all the challenges of this closeness so real, so visible and palpable. To feed on the word of God is to be filled with a deep desire to do His will and in no way to prevent God's will from being truly fulfilled in fullness among us. In the Gospel of St. Luke, 22, 24, we find Jesus in deep agony in the Mount of Olives. Jesus was like the child on the river bank, it is obvious that Jesus was afraid in that moment of agony, Jesus brings upon himself the agony of the agonizing world and tested by the yoke of wickedness, sin and disobedience, Jesus felt upon him the painful burden of an infamous and disobedient humanity. Jesus wept and Jesus sweated drops of blood that dripped on the ground.

Listen carefully, all this may seem an exercise of simple ability, but to follow Christ means to confront ourselves directly with the original truth and that is nourishment, because to recognize our history, even if it is frightening and painful, nourishes us with courage to make the most appropriate decision towards ourselves and our future. Only he who understands what he truly needs can be nourished. *Angels live in fullness because they are angels and were made for the glory of God and they do exactly what God wants.* Humanity suffers from the original taint and this has destroyed the harmony between the soul and the spirit, between the physical and the spiritual. Within each one of us there are disordered desires, there is a corruption that is constantly subordinated to the tyranny of a decadent, distorted and depressed nature, so do not be frightened when you begin to realize all that is in you and that has existed for many years, but that before approaching Christ all that was hidden in the rubble of your dense voids and false structures.

To follow Christ means to know how to get out of the trap of these dark cellars, it is to overcome the fear of facing oneself, it is to open oneself to the possibility of leaving the past in the past and no longer judging and condemning oneself, to definitely begin a real journey towards the liberating light of the person and of the mercy that comes from Jesus Christ.

May our sins not be the reason for our despair, but the reason that drives us to the real search for our faith. We have all failed, fallen, hit rock bottom, even the saints in the process of sanctification went through these depressing experiences, they were tempted and wounded, but through the integrity of obedience, to faith and retraining in the grace of God, they were able, through repentance, to get up again and start again on the path of God. *If you want to nourish yourself and be a person willing to be a witness of God's grace, you must understand that each day has its beginning and its end, in it is reflected the full existence of the one who lived today in the fullness of faith without losing the hope of overcoming and spiritual progress. The one who surrenders to Christ begins to attain the grace of wisdom, the faculty of knowledge of spiritual things and the potential gift that makes us see things, understand them and be able to interpret them, not with the fallen vision of humanity, but with the supernatural understanding of the will of God through the Holy Spirit.* I invite you to pray in the power of the Holy Spirit, to enter into deep prayer of intimacy wherever you are, just connect your heart and mind with the presence of God. Enter through your prayer into the hiddenness of God and allow Him to open your mind even more to the things that you humanly fail to understand and for which perhaps, you are suffering. A humble prayer can lift us into God's loving presence, help us overcome chains and free us from the many machinations to which the evil enemy wants to bind us. Prayer fills us with light and guides our journey. *Wisdom is not knowing more than others, wisdom is knowing and seeing exactly what God wants us to know and see, a wise man cannot be wiser than the wisdom of God, the wisdom of the wise is limited to the ineffable knowledge that comes from the high heavens.*

God gives us the vision, but he has the foresight, he is the God who provides, who will always see first and supply each one of us. The wise man is the one who decides to follow Christ and in this following discovers his neighbor and learns to love, respect, understand and lift him up, the wise man is the one who helps with love to heal his neighbor of his wounds and with deep compassion gives himself the opportunity to forgive him. The wise is the one who understands that his fellow man, the one who is close to you, is the intact manifestation of the divine creator, the wisdom that comes down from the high heavens and enters our hearts; it allows us to see, feel and understand that the person who makes you suffer, no matter how unpleasant he may be to your understanding, is the image and likeness of the almighty and needs healing, intercession and prayer to overcome and be different. This wisdom teaches us to crucify our flesh and our passions in Christ, this is the mystery of our faith. *"For those who belong to Christ Jesus have crucified the flesh with its passions and desires. If we live by the Spirit, let us also walk by the Spirit…"* (**Galatians 5:24**).

Still speaking of the following of Christ, I could not fail to quote the Apostle Paul, in all his writings, in his letters, we can find his great and profound motives considering the countless efforts to remain faithful in the following of Christ. For Paul, following Christ was much more than a necessity, but rather a definitive decision of his existence since his encounter with Jesus on the road to Damascus, in the mission that God entrusted to him, required him to accept a total resignation of self. *Thus, Paul's emphasis on faith made him observe that all great spiritual feats could be experienced if they were really necessary for God.* For the apostle Paul, the word of God is manifested in us in works and repeated tolls, vigils of prayer, famine, abundance of goods, thirst, fasting, cold and calamities (cf. 2 Corinthians 11:27). To make effective the growth of his following of Christ, Paul understood the need for a life nourished by spiritual strength, through his own exercises of faith; for him, his spiritual life was compared to the Olympics. *"Those who run in the stadium run all together, but only one attains the prize, run therefore, so that you may be victorious and he who prepares himself for the fight abstains from everything and this resignation does so in order to attain a corruptible crown, yet we, in all our exercises of faith toward spirituality, run in order to attain an incorruptible crown."* (**1 Corinthians 9:24,25**). The apostle Paul was not running without direction, he knew perfectly well, since the day of his encounter with Christ on the road to Damascus, the meaning of his battle. He knew that only in Christ could he fulfill the fullness of his existence, that is why he himself said: *"I do not fight as one who fights with the air, but I chasten and educate my body under the healthy dominion of grace so that it does not happen that, having been myself a proclaimer of Christ to others, I will be reproved for my unworthiness"* (**1 Corinthians, 9:26,27**).

It is clear to understand that Paul chose to live this way because he considered that it was not easy to reach the pinnacle of spiritual perfection, but he had it clear in his faith and, through the experience of his encounter with Christ, a fire was burning in his heart to attain it. In memory now of St. Augustine, who explicitly reveals and declares in his writings in the book of The Confessions: *"My heart you made yours, my Lord, and my heart will be restless until it rests in you".* It is this desire for God that makes us capable of understanding the real need to live in Christ, this was also the same experience of the disciples on the road to Emmaus, when upon encountering Christ and listening to his words, felt in their hearts the ardor of the liberating truth that can only be discovered and felt in Christ Jesus.

St. Paul tells us: *"I do not pretend to tell you that I have already attained perfection, but I put my strength to attain it once I myself was first conquered by Christ Jesus. Brethren, aware that I have not yet conquered it, I seek only one thing, forgetting what lies behind, I run in pursuit of what lies ahead, I run to reach the goal, to take possession of the crown of the vocation on the heights of God in Christ Jesus and all of us who are nourished by the ideal of perfection, let us have these same sentiments. And if you feel otherwise, only God can clarify it. In any case, whatever the point already reached, what matters is to continue always under the same vision, towards the same direction. Therefore, brethren, be my imitators, and look to those who live according to the pattern we have shown you.* (Philippians 3:12-17).

Without a doubt, Paul understood the true meaning of following Christ. For many leaders of our time: popes, bishops, priests, pastors, ministers, evangelists, leaders of the schools of faith, and the laity in general, it is still a challenge to understand the following of Christ. Many of us, from the many institutions of faith and biblical teaching, countless congregations, prayer assemblies, leaders of academic institutions, still find ourselves immersed in mere fundamentalisms and human doctrines far removed from the true following of Christ in the light of truth. *Paul became a slave and completely gave himself to doing nothing that would not lead him to the definitive course of Christ.* That is why he wrote: *"I urge you, by the mercy of God, to offer yourselves as a living sacrifice, holy and acceptable to God, this will be your true spiritual worship".* (Romans. 12,1).

From our surrender, from our untiring sacrifice of love, we will begin to discover in ourselves, in our mind and heart transformed in the light of education by obedience to the word of God, the sense of following Christ, not by perfection, but by the untiring desire to reach it.

It is like the child who, while traveling towards the river without having seen it, already imagines, feels, enjoys and longs for the feel of its waters.

It is very important that you understand that all this struggle, this search and this desire, come from a soul that is really living the experience of the exodus, of the journey, of the exit from a static life to a dynamic life by the Holy Spirit. A person who is inert, empty, closed in on himself without desire or longing for Christ, will never be able to understand the meaning of the word search. *The search is part of the spiritual process, because it is the one that causes us the appetite and the dependent need to seek in Christ*, what truly does not exist in us and in any other part of the orb of creation, **the creature, to be satisfied, needs creation, but in God, the man of God needs Christ.** Christ was not created, Christ being God begotten, makes us find in his love the fullness of all that cannot be found in ourselves and in every work of the natural God. Therefore, enjoying Christ, who is not a creature, but equal to the Father, full of the same nature, each one of us, by seeking him, by experiencing him, in the encounter of faith in the mystery of the sacrament, can enjoy how great, how glorious, how sweet, how tasty and immensely wonderful is the Lord Jesus Christ, the only Son of God.

Let us definitely not be afraid of this exalted intimacy. To contemplate Christ through the sacrament of the Eucharist is an undoubtedly real grace. His presence is in body, blood, soul and divinity, and as we approach the blissful banquet, we are blessed by the privilege of being able to enter into such copious communion. Young people need to discover the power of the Eucharist, its healing power and its rapturous power. It is the task of all of us to unite around the altar and desire to eat of the body and drink of the precious blood of Jesus Christ.

If something prevents you from experiencing Christ in this dimension, this something must be immediately chosen not to be part of your existence. If you truly want to be part of the body of Jesus Christ, everything that prevents you from communion with Christ, is something that limits your life and makes you infertile and weak.

Following Christ grants us the power to mix our existence with the power of his efficacy, that is to say, it is no longer I who live, but every part of our existence is taken, dominated and oriented by the grace and real essence of Jesus Christ, that is why we can be called Christians. This is why we must give the world the opportunity to enjoy through us the sweetness of Christ, in this way our life must be classified, crucified and resurrected in the mystery of love.

Perhaps this language seems to you very sublime, even unattainable from your personal point of view towards yourself and towards the people who are around you in your daily life. But I would now like to encourage you in faith and make you understand that none of us are in any way excluded from this beautiful and marvelous grace. You do not need to be a theologian or a person dedicated through a consecrated vocation as a priest or religious to understand this wisdom that is not revealed to the great and the wise of this earth in this time in which we live, but this divine sweetness, this pleasant taste of God, is revealed to those who are ready to the true renunciation and commitment to reach purity of heart. It is to the simple soul that God reveals the unfathomable greatness of his love. **He does not call the able, but enables them by the call, it is the exercise of his work of love.**

The truth found in the scriptures of God's word leads us to the challenge of the imitation of Christ as a priority of faith, as a way of redemption and liberation. Many still prefer to follow bad examples, to live according to evil, to consider a life of corruption and lies in order to take advantage. They seek a way of existence where wickedness and carnal vices end up leading them to despair. It must never be forgotten that a lie taken as truth can never become truth. The path of perversion has no way back because of the error itself. The only way to overcome this great lie that blinds the understanding and makes the human being vulnerable, is the rescue by repentance and the desire to live a new life in Christ. *"Carrying our own cross and following Him with our own truth of existing, putting aside what is not worthy of Him and resolutely assuming in us what He dignifies us for a new life."* (Matthew 10:38).

When the disciples asked Jesus how anyone could be saved and redeemed, Jesus answered them: *"Strive to enter the narrow gate, for many will try, but will not succeed".* (Luke 13:24). *"The kingdom of heaven suffers violence, and it is the violent who conquer by force."* (Matthew 11:12). *"Seek first the kingdom and all its righteousness and all else will be given to you as well."* (Matthew 6:33). Every spiritual process must be consistent with the inner attitude in its desire and virtue. The external efforts, in their moral, ethical and aesthetic change, that is to say, not only to wash the outside of the jar and leave it dirty on the inside. It is more than necessary to clean from the outside in and from the inside out and only when one is truly clean, then one is able to receive the new life in Christ Jesus. *"No one puts new oil into old vessels, but new oil, new wine, new life, for new vessels."* (Mark 2:22). If you really want to achieve this real grace of God's life being lived in us, do not wait any longer, start now, the time is now, your opportunity has come. *Seeking God is an extraordinary work, everything brings us closer in a great way when we allow our being to walk towards the greatness of God. The vision is enlarged, the feelings are restored and positivized, the words become clearer and more forceful and our ideas become more respected, all this because we assume the life of Christ in us and the very presence of Christ is in charge of making us great and visibly abundant men* when we make the decision to live from Him, to live only in Him, with Him, for Him, without abstracting ourselves from loving the most deprived neighbor beside us.

To live in Christ is to penetrate into God, to take refuge and be nourished by his love, to develop a spiritual life has nothing to do with alienation from the world, fanaticism and illusionism. It is not the denial of existence or of our capacities, much less of the faculties given to us by God, it is not to renounce our neighbor and isolate ourselves by pretending to live an exclusive, vain and selfish life.

The relationship with God is a relationship as the first commandment invites us, *to love Him above all things and our neighbor as ourselves*, that is, it will be impossible to love God without discovering Him in my life and my life in Him, and the consequence of this love will produce the reflection of compassion and the desire to share with my neighbor this wonderful grace. This new way of relating, unmasks and removes from us, man, woman and integral human being, the desire for the prevalence of one over the other, we discover that we are not islands and if this is how we find ourselves at this moment with our own reality, we realize that we can only grow if we unite and add forces and capacities. *For this marvelous collective task we have the cross of Christ, which is the necessary bridge to unite us with one another in the same heart, in the same love and in the same desire.* Nor will this take away from us the exclusive originality of our creation; **we are unique and unrepeatable people because God wanted to imprint on the creation of the human being an exclusive character in his image and likeness, precisely so that love could realize its excellence in being love, not in itself, but in communion with the other.** The realization of God's grace in us is in that we first love each other, love ourselves, forgive ourselves, cherish ourselves; it is an exhaustive process of healing, of transformation and realization, he who seeks to be loved before desiring to love himself, loses himself, he who wants to be loved finds the fullness of love in God's own love. *"For God so loved the world that he sent us his only begotten son so that whoever believes may live forever."* (**John 3:16**). Self-centered, individualistic, selfish, super self-sufficient love is not love, it is a deceitful passion that invades the mind and heart and hinders nature, leading the person to commit unhealthy acts of great danger to his own life and to the lives of others.

Can you imagine the meaning of this love that comes into your life in a God-sent way? It is an invitation to be transformed when we understand this grace in our lives and in the lives of those around us. Thus experienced those who lived close to the Virgin Mary, mother of Jesus, to be able to see in her an extremely blessed and grateful woman. When the angel Gabriel came to her saying that by God she had been chosen to be the mother of his son, to be the bearer of the incarnation of God's own son to men and that she was full of grace, she could begin to understand the meaning, not of a supposedly human greatness of her as a person, but she could begin to understand the power of her mission as God's chosen one to carry in her womb the "Word", God himself made flesh for the salvation of all mankind. Then she proclaimed: *"My soul magnifies the Lord and my spirit exults for joy in God my Savior, holy is his name"* (**Luke 1:46**). In this same prayer, the Virgin Mary acknowledges the beatitude that encompasses her existence, she recognizes the enormous work of God in her own existence, she sings of God's favors and submits herself to his authority. Each of us, in understanding this profound manifestation of God and His love revealed to our hearts, must also understand the power of the beatitude that exists in our existence, we are not left to our own devices, as some believe. There is in us an inner code of bliss, it is enough that we wholeheartedly desire to assume this great divine gift. We are invited to fill ourselves with inner joy, to assume a life of happiness and liberation, to glorify God with our acts, thoughts and everything that potentially exists in our existence. Be like Mary, a blessed one, and rejoice every moment in the Lord.

To be blessed is not to enjoy a title, but a real condition in one's own life, this experience can be found in the scenario of Mary's visitation to her cousin Elizabeth. Mary, full of grace, bearer of Christ by the grace of the Holy Spirit, arrives at her cousin's house, not to boast of the deeds of God in her existence, but she arrives at Elizabeth's house to offer service, support and donation of her time, of her youth, of her own life. Upon her arrival, Mary is surprised by Elizabeth's greeting when she realizes that her cousin recognizes in her the manifestation of the Almighty and names her mother of her lord. Elizabeth automatically feels unworthy of such a great visitation, despite the fact that Mary has not said any word of the child in her womb, Elizabeth jumped for joy, John the Baptist recognizes the arrival of the one who he should announce and should prepare the way in the desert for. That is why he jumped for joy, of interior prostration in the womb of his mother Elizabeth. This is exactly what we are trying to share through this teaching, allow yourself to be filled with God's grace, with the excellence of God's visitation within you, this same grace that took possession of your existence will manifest to others the power of love present within them. Your life will be an effective instrument of God for others to find answers and meaning to many problems and dilemmas. In this way never believe that the work is yours, do not be fooled into believing that everything is under your personal control, the work is God's, he works all the time, we will always be happy as long as we dedicate ourselves to be imitators of Christ and bearers of the grace of heaven. Let us let God work in us and let us keep our lives in his divine will.

When St. Paul speaks to us about the goal and that our goal should be to follow Christ, he is speaking directly to all those who have already made the option of choosing the narrow gate and have the coherence to understand that whoever chose Christ, chose the better part and that this part will never be taken away from him. But it is important to understand that choosing Christ is choosing the road from Bethlehem to Jerusalem, that is, it is choosing to live each step of Christ's life, from the moment of his birth in the portal of Bethlehem, to his passion and his resurrection in Jerusalem. Unfortunately many seek beatitude, but forget the essential steps to be truly blessed. Mary, from the moment of conception until Pentecost, knew how to understand the integrity of her mission with Jesus among men by the apostles and among the apostles, *her silence was not selfish or omissive but a wise sign of one who, by mission, had been chosen not to speak, but to execute the word of God.* Here we find a great teaching for our discipline in the education of the faith: if we wish to reach the goal, one of the ways to nourish our spiritual life is to learn through our spiritual life together to have fruitful times for listening to God. St. Benedict, at the beginning of the spiritual rule of life for the monks of his monastery, begins by inviting them to **listen to the teachings of the master**. If we really paid attention to how much God has to say to us, we would easily understand that there is little need to speak when we, through our actions, once healed by God, can easily and widely communicate the beatitudes of the effects of his love in our own lives, that is, to bear witness, to speak coherently of the works of God directly manifested to us.

In the morning sermon we find Jesus humbly seated on a stone, with deep love and teaching he communicated to all the listeners the possibility of understanding, of the true purpose of discovering oneself a blessed one, Jesus opens their understanding making them see what could really make them differentiated and blessed men and women. "Blessed are the poor in spirit, those who mourn, for they shall be comforted; the meek, for they shall inherit the earth; those who hunger and thirst for righteousness, for they shall be satisfied; the merciful, for they shall obtain mercy; the pure in heart, for they shall see God; the peacemakers, for they shall be called children of God; those who are persecuted for righteousness' sake, for theirs is the kingdom of heaven". This entire teaching wants to tell us and orient us towards only one thing: that it is necessary for Christ to grow in us and for us to diminish in ourselves, so that we understand that to be blessed is, more than anything else, to assume the goal of the mission in the Lord. We were not created for a lazy, inconsistent life with no consequential implications. Each of us came into this existence to make history and to reflect God's will for the good of humanity. That is why we enjoy so many favors, gifts, charisms and possibilities. God's love was communicated and given to us so that we can produce abundant fruits of satisfaction and great profit. All this we will achieve through obedience of life, to the word of God, through the excellence of prayer and true love shared with one another.

The greatest examples of spirituality, the men and women who sanctified themselves through an integral life of prayer, always reflected in themselves a luminous and happy state of mind. We could mention some of them: St. Francis of Assisi, St. Therese of the Child Jesus, St. Teresa the Great, St. John of the Cross, St. Rita of Cascia, St. Padre Pio, St. Gemma Galgani, and so many others who followed the path, were able to find inner peace, the glorious joy of what it is to enjoy a blessed and successful life in the field of spirituality. I would like you to understand that a person who lives worthily in the light of the truth in the most multiple professions that your mind can reach, can also perfectly enjoy the abundance of being a blessed one. He need not be exclusively consecrated to the ministerial or vocational life. To be blessed is not only and exclusively a privilege of a few. *The beatitude and the power to become blessed is a gradual exercise of surrender to God, to his teaching and to the complete fulfillment of the acceptance of his divine will.*

Some years ago, I made friends with a man I met at the airport, I was traveling from Rio de Janeiro to New York and he was in the same boarding lounge, he was traveling to the same destination. Our flight had a delay of 4 hours due to a maintenance that had to be done on the plane. While I was waiting in the waiting room, my attention was drawn to that man who, very crestfallen, almost hiding inside his seat in an attitude of deep sadness, it was possible to feel his state of soul totally defeated and without strength. Since you know me and how I am and the way God uses me, I felt the impetus and the strength full of desire to approach him and start a conversation that could somehow bring him God's healing. Immediately I got up and sat down two chairs away from where he was, I began to look at him and he noticed the fixed look in my eyes and by far, the Holy Spirit touched him to come and talk to me. In that instant I felt that I began to manifest a great moment of grace and miracle. Without the man saying a single word to me, I had a vision of a house being swallowed by the earth, I had the discernment that the suffering of that man had to do with a great misfortune that was happening in his life and his home and I told him the vision I had, which caused him to be amazed and to break down in tears. **The end of the story was not only the man's realization of what he had done wrong and what he had to ask forgiveness from his family for, but it was the exact realization that a person cannot pretend to achieve everything on their own.** The man's greatest problem was his isolation in himself, in his powers and capacities, in his salary, in his position in his company, in his human advantages, totally forgetting his inner need for God and in recognizing that in spite of his human goals, each one of us will only reach the fullness of our existence by discovering the essential goal which is Christ. Many have everything and at the same time have nothing. The emptiness remains because nothing fills them internally, hence so much sadness, disappointments, depressions and moral failures. As long as you barely want to achieve your human goals, your life will always be a place of misunderstandings, disasters, mismatches and losses. All this happens because it is impossible to satisfy oneself from the creature and creation. ***Our goal is integral satisfaction through the grace of God***, when we put ourselves at the service, not only of ourselves but also of each other, that is to reach the meaning of a blessed life.

Before your eyes, in front of you, within the reach of your hands, are two paths, one totally unknown, but with immense and eternal possibilities and another duly recognized of success, fame and prestige, but without any pretense of the possibility that you will have to put everything on your side and fight against all. This dualism seems to be deeply irresistible in the two options. The first, the unknown is the path that causes us fear, but also incites us to adventure, to the inner challenge of reaching beyond. The second is the predictable path but very prone to arrogance, conceit, pride and vanity. Choosing the right and effective path is the beginning of the true end as the meaning and goal of life. The way that Christ offers us is the first, the way that leads us to God. If it is necessary to know, if it is necessary to discover, if it is necessary to penetrate and enter into his intimacy, on God's way nothing is done because everything will be done with Him, in Him and through Him. On the second path are the tragedies, the losses, the failures that others have left in the middle and you will have to put a lot of effort and undertake a lot of human energy to make things happen your way or resign yourself to accept unfinished works and frustrated possibilities. Many reach, but they are never fulfilled. In God's way, every step, every feeling, every expression, every decision, every strategy, will have to be ordered under God's will and His teaching, because the most important thing we must learn in the field of faith is to **listen** to God and exercise obedience. Without belittling oneself, always be ready to contemplate the goal and the individual capacity within. In the first way all things are concrete, because the house is being built, the personality is being formed by the grace of God on the rock that is Christ, the cornerstone. In contrast, in the second way all things seem to be ready-made, at hand, very well designed, definitely easily built, the structures are very formal and seem indestructible. Then, if the person chooses corruption, lies and vices, it seems to be easier, but the big difference is that this structure is built on weak foundations, on sand and then is when the problems begin, the winds and tribulations, pains, diseases and severe difficulties, nothing stays, everything collapses and it is necessary to start all over again with many more difficulties. *We must not work only with the power of ease, but with the power of intelligence and wisdom. The things that truly remain in our lives are those that take strength, effort, work, sacrifice and above all, time. Therefore, when we achieve them, they become very valuable. However, the things that are apparently easy, such as frauds, corruptions, act in the middle of the night and then appear in the morning, but as they arrive, so they leave, because they do not have the dignity of the work of a whole existence kept under the will of God.* All your efforts, which are innumerable, will be the beginning of success because you have chosen the right path.

The one who chooses the first path is the one who chooses the narrow door and he did it because he understands that each of his choices will have to be classified and accepted at the pace of his personal history. Everything is well placed in the eyes of the God in blessing. *Nothing is alien to his knowledge and no one but God knows all the sacrifices we make and whether we make them in the light of truth.* He who chooses the second way, chooses the wide door in which everything, exactly everything, enters disorderly, without any classification to be ordered, do you understand now the difference between the two doors? It is you who must know which of the two you want to choose to enter. You already know exactly the pros and cons of the two, the most important thing is that you are not deceiving yourself and if you are wrong, there is still a favorable time to start again and become blessed.

God helps us and guides us in every possible way to make us overcome difficulties, but what God cannot do is to assume what is proper to each one of us. What depends on supernatural action will be fully and perfectly accomplished in due time. God works and will continue to work so that his work is complete in us, **God is faithful**. But what depends upon natural action, that is, upon our deeds, decisions, commitments and direct actions, will have to be observed, sorted out and ordered through the proven virtues and an authentic faith in the following of Christ. Each one must assume his part in the process of becoming a better person, a better human being, willing to improve and develop a more effective existence in the universe. It becomes necessary the manifestation of the excellent values that each one can develop in Christ in order to reach what is good, pleasant, holy and classifiable in the eyes of God **(Galatians 5)**. If you only want to exclusively fulfill your ephemeral desires, you will have a miserable life, but if you decide to take the path towards the entrance of the narrow gate, understanding the challenges and assuming by faith all the commitments, the possibility of overcoming and growing, is unquestionably real and concrete, certainly, fulfilling all the requirements and keeping persevering, you will come out victorious.

"Lift up your weary hands and bend your trembling knees." **(Hebrews, 12.12)**. Every man, every woman, every integral human being who decides to enter through the narrow gate, must not lose sight of the importance of prayer, which for us, in the program of spiritual nourishment, is the daily food of great value. Whoever wants to come closer to Christ, imitate him and enjoy his love, must have in view the goal that is not only made along the way, but in every step and new discovery towards itself, that is, *it is not only to look at something that is far away and wish to reach it, but to have the vision set in every action, thought, word, deed and even omissions, which make us think and refer directly to the understanding of our personality towards our goals of attainment.* Each person, in the desire to get closer to Christ, needs to realize the mismatch in their way of thinking, speaking, acting, even in the great cowardice not to assume their own weaknesses, this is what causes the great difficulty in following Christ, the absence and non-acceptance of this need to have a transformed personality and personified in the person of Christ, can become very painful in every process.

Remember that what you are, can always be changed. God's grace in us made us unrepeatable, unique, but that does not mean that we should not be improved and transformed. A good example is found in the word of God concerning the potter's house: *"Can I not make you like this potter, a house in Israel?"* **(Jeremiah 18:6)**. The vessel is unique, but that does not detract from the potter's freedom to make it new as many times as necessary. Every morning, as the Lord's mercy is renewed in our lives, so must you and I seek renewal. We must seek the favorable means to be disposed to the grace of attaining transformation. I am certain that we can achieve the healthy and spiritual improvement of our personality. Perhaps the best example

I can give you in the Bible about this is the life of Mary Magdalene, an enthusiastic, creative, beautiful woman, different from the other women of her time, but undoubtedly a woman who had chosen the wide door, she had everything in her life, but at the same time she did not have the freedom to be happy, certainly she had to be confronted in an abusive way to the miserable judgment of those who took advantage of her for a while and now presented her as dirty and undeserving to continue living. The encounter with Jesus, at the moment when she encountered the narrow door, made her understand in a full and effective way that it was not only her moral habits that needed to be changed, but also her own personality, her inner self, her values, everything that was stuck in the most sensitive part of her existence. She contemplated in her being how fully she would leave the slavery of sin, to assume now the real and true lordship of the person of Christ. Mary Magdalene was forgiven much, but she had much love and perhaps the love of this sinner, to this day, is difficult to be understood, because many of us are not willing to throw ourselves and submit ourselves in the exercise towards the high levels in which she knew how to love. To heal the personality is to allow oneself not only to start a new life, but to allow oneself to become a new person, rediscovering in yourself a new life potential, new values and possibilities, leaving fears behind and opening to new horizons in Christ Jesus; a new creature, with a transformed personality and a changed way of thinking, enjoying the integrity of Christ's dwelling place. ***Do not tire of lifting up your hands and bending your knees before him who is almighty***, only Christ can reinterpret our history, only he can give us back all that was stolen from us by Satan, only he can assure us fullness of victory and free us from all condemnation. I am absolutely sure that you have fallen many times in your life and out of ignorance you have raised your hands to unnecessary things and looked for help in the wrong places; that because of the fragility of faith, you have prostrated your body before demons that tried to destroy you. ***But I am even more certain that if today you would understand the greatness of following Christ, the greatness of discovering his love, the power of his grace and truly assume the commitment to be blessed, you will definitely become a different person, nourished by the real potential of faith. Do not be afraid to reach this proximity to the springs of life in the spirit, let yourself be filled by the new waters of God, of his permanent anointing that invigorates you again through the forgiveness that only he can give you, because only he can make you a faithful instrument of beatitude on the face of the earth.***

III. God's unforgettable love

"Whoever does not love does not know God, for God is love." 1 John 4:8

In these dark times that we have lived, perhaps times of deep miserability of values, of the senses of the same capacity of perception around us, the whole of humanity is submerged in great darkness of subjectivity, consumerism and hedonism. This darkness, despite being extremely confusing and capable of weakening any effective action of our life, allows itself to be illuminated by the inconsequential and disturbing reflections of life that mostly come from the absurd proposals of distraction and false illusions of lies that seek to confuse the most vulnerable. The world is asleep in the darkness of ignorance, although philosophy tells us that ignorance is the beginning of the teaching process towards wisdom, the darkness we are referring to is the dense darkness of abandonment, of rejection, of deafness, of the same idleness that traps all humanity to remain enslaved and afraid to discover the magnificent and splendorous light of the truth that shines in Christ. **The world wants to deny Christ, because it does not want to access the light.** This is the worst mistake.

God is an infinite sea, an unfathomable ocean capable of reaching the most hidden corners of the room of all ignorance to offer the abundance of his presence, from the greatest to the smallest. Perhaps what you can imagine knowing the most insignificant, the meaningless, even the expressionless, that which one has declassified as unnecessary in the light of your understanding, all that is visible, even that which is invisible, every molecule of being, every atom. *Everything that happens in the universe is the imponderable work of an immense illuminated, glorious, full and eternal love, capable of dissipating, in a single instant, any level of darkness, and that love is God himself.* All that is incomprehensible and inscrutable is yet encompassable by his eternal wisdom. **Thus, each of us is invited to understand that no matter how strong we may be, it will still be insufficient to limit God in our concepts, God is unfathomable, that is the beautiful truth that carries our greatest assurance of faith.** However, his divine power is capable of embracing creation with a profound stroke of infinite goodness and mercy. The magnificence of his love exceeds all ignorance, all acts of rebellion, all crimes, human miseries, sins and infractions. Even his love embraces all that is still resistant to faith, by which I mean that God's love embraces even those who are not yet able to believe in him. Definitely, only God's love can reach the simplest and the most complex of humanity.

This is what his word warns us when he reveals to us that God does not make *"exceptions of people"* **(Acts 10:34).** God is incapable of making fun of our situations, even the most miserable or marginal ones. He, with profound goodness, descends to our situation, no matter how bad it may be, and comes to the aid of our condition, even if it is not favorable. He contemplates our personal history and *his love, which is sovereignly capable of drawing in us a new expression, a new character, his compassionate power, imprints on our being obscured by darkness a transformed and vivified personality full of dignity.*

It was God's own love that brought us out of non-existence. A pain we bring, a problem we have, a wrong step we take, a disappointment, a frustration, a deception, a betrayal, all these things, when they happen, seem to reduce us to absolutely nothing. It is perceptible the disorder that this feeling causes, not only in our material body, but also in our emotions, in our psyche; it is what we call disappointing and debilitating frustration. However, the non-existence from which we were taken, can never be compared to the nothingness of human consciousness. For man nothingness will always be negative, for God nothingness is the full beginning of the beginning of creation, we were not removed from a negative extract nor were we created from a miserable non-existence. We came out of the depths of the image and likeness of God, which can never be compared to an impotent morbid non-existence. To come out of God, to come out of his image and likeness, is to come out of a reality unknown to matter, but fully and profoundly real in the eternal womb of the Most Holy Trinity **(Gen 1:26).** We are not just any work, our weaknesses are the root of sin and rebellion. We maintain within us an intact reality that is the image and likeness of our Creator.

A great artist, perhaps one of the greatest artists of humanity, after having finished his great work, which in a spectacular way he had molded from an immense rock, all his admirers asked: **"How could you create something so great and wonderful?"** and the artist with all his humility answered: **"I did not create anything, all this beauty already existed inside the rock, I only removed the excesses so that it could be seen as it was".**

If an artist can remove excesses and make his work translucent in such a simple way, how will God's love not be able to reveal through us what already existed in its depths? We can thus say that we are not the work of nothingness, the character of the image and likeness of God is the most worthy and real expression of the love that was embedded from all eternity in the creative principle of the essence, matter, substance and will of the divine immensity. **Only a loving God in supreme form, could embody love in the form of creation. So then, God's creative work is the most eloquent cry of love and the manifestation of the beloved towards his be-**

loved. How can we deny this love? How can we continue to mock love? Why so much selfishness, why so much hatred, so much resentment, so much bitterness and so much vandalism? Why so much destruction, so many aberrations, trying to stain this ineffable work of profound love. *Perhaps in this life and up to this moment, no one has made you understand how much genuine love there is in every atom of your existence. Perhaps your life experiences, the traumas, the frustrations, the evils you have suffered, the absences you have had to face, in one way or another made you believe that love is an unattainable illusion, a romantic invention of fools, of the most fragile, of the intellectually weak and even of a manipulative religion.* But the love that I want to present at this moment does not compare to any love revealed on the face of the earth, I am fully convinced that the strict and only way for the healing of all these evils that have deeply wounded you, is found in the illumination and real discovery of the love that exceeds all loves, which is called love creator of God.

Jesus, upon meeting Nicodemus, perceives in his character and personality that in spite of the fact that he was already an old man and that Nicodemus had already experienced all the tastes and sorrows of a life of many positive and negative actions, he also perceives that within him there was still a great expectation of something more, a desperate longing for answers and a soul full of questions. The fact that Nicodemus, a worthy man of the Jewish society, sought an encounter with Christ in the garden, in the late hours of the night, undoubtedly refers us to the search of someone who at the same time and with a certain fear, wanted to know the true light and who definitely recognizes in Jesus this power. Once again I feel the need to intrude and invite you to allow yourself to see a reflection of the life of Nicodemus and his experience with Christ. Perhaps up to today you have lived a trajectory very similar to that of this man in the Gospel story, ups, downs, encounters, misunderstandings, losses, gains, but you still lack in the garden of silence, in the middle of the dark night, when you alone are before your own conscience, to receive the special visit of Jesus and be able to share with him all his questions and anxieties, you will certainly come out different. Jesus, looking at Nicodemus, found reflected in his posture the gentleness of a person, but at the same time his longing for transformation and Jesus looking at him with deep compassion, wanted to reveal to him the secret of the creator to creature. Jesus said to Nicodemus: *"You need only one thing*, no more weight, no more hours of work, no more goods, no more weariness, no more human intelligence, no more status and positions of power, the one and only thing you need is: *to be born again"*. This word of Jesus, this simple secret, but of great power, troubled the soul of Nicodemus, to the point that he himself, still shrouded in darkness, asked Jesus, *"How can I, an old man, return to my mother's womb?"* Exactly in this way, with this same confusion of Nicodemus, we continue to inquire about God wrongly, I do not know if we are foolish or want to believe that it is God who is proposing something absurd. Many of us are not capable of perceiving the kind proposals of God, it is easy for us to continue with our interrogations, we continue with our incapable, improper, unnecessary proposals, which are nothing more than unfounded justifications to deny the powerful force of the creator before us, his creations. Jesus, with the power of grace, with the authority given to him by the Father, says penetratingly to Nicodemus: **"He who is not born of water and the Spirit can never live fully"** and Jesus added: **"The Spirit, Nicodemus, blows where He wills"**.

If you want to enter into this mystery of God's love, you must fight to overcome every state of misery, of oppression, of domination, of slavery, all that you bring within you that robs you of your will, that fills you with idleness, that does not allow you to get up, that brings you trapped in its vices and disturbances, all that makes you lose the way to the light. *The time is ripe and the time has come for you to allow your soul to be taken by the new birth, the birth by the power and efficacy of the Holy Spirit.*

Only the man and the woman who are healed by the Holy Spirit can be born again, be a new creature, stop being a vessel full of hatred, full of wounds of trampled blood, to receive the springs of the living and purifying waters capable of bringing to life, the newness of God. The new birth is not a material, circumstantial work, it is, explicitly, the spiritual rebirth, now life, cleansed of the vicissitudes of the satanic inheritance of sin, is reborn to fullness of light in Christ Jesus.

In Christ Jesus we are new creatures and he who receives this new birth, can really feel the difference of a life lived in disgrace and now in the abundance of life in God, who fills us with grace. May you understand that being born again is not a mere invitation, but more than anything else, it is God's most eloquent challenge to each one of us to enter into the mystery of the new life, the life of love, the life of blessing. *If the father or mother think they are very important because they have been able to have a son or daughter, they will feel even more important when they realize that only God can make children be born again through a spiritual pregnancy by faith, by transformation, by gifts, by charisms, by the ineffable power of the Holy Spirit.*

Many of your children are lost and disoriented, or have been damaged by the defilements of this world, precisely because you yourselves have aborted in them the power of faith, the power of the Holy Spirit, the power of the teaching of the word of God. You yourselves were to blame for the fact that your children today renounce and deny the existence of God. It was the separation of spiritual values, the time you refused to assist your lives with the power of faith. It was also the denial of time to attend the life of spiritual teaching, it was the excessive work and the unbridled passion for vices that separated them from the discipline of faith, from the life in community and from prayer itself. All this will cause the family to be subjected to an immense spiritual ignorance and an abyss far from the faith, perhaps there was abundance in everything, but misery of God, of values and virtues consequent of intimacy with Christ. *You are also responsible so that now, by the strength and grace of God for your children, you assume the commitment to prophesy in your homes the new breath of Pentecost, to pray with faith with hands raised, knees bent, so that your children, like Nicodemus, have the opportunity to be born again and be filled with the spirit of God.* Fathers and mothers, make a commitment to pray for your families, to restore them, to do the maximum possible and impossible so that your homes may be transformed into a hall of praise and spiritual learning towards the new birth in faith. May they be immersed in this grace of leaving the old man, the old life, the old structures, the old covenants, in order to accept the constant fullness of the new life, now nourished not only by isolated rites, but by a concrete and enlightened following of the word of God. *I challenge them to begin to discover the power of the Bible, of the teaching that comes to us from God's own word. Take home a giant screen, the powerful word of God. Teach through it that your family can be nourished through the most beautiful and healing stories that reflect the move of God on the face of the earth. The Bible is the word of God sown in our hearts, powerful to dissipate every knot and disrupt every mental conflict we have, to set us on the path of deep love for God, to heal and free us from every vice and curse. The word of God is the exalted spring that always gushes and flows in our hearts, the desire for a worthy and sanctified life, it is the word that impels us towards the miracles and fruitfulness of a life faithful to God and extended to the service and charity offered to one another.*

Will you be able or fit and worthy enough to describe in all its richness of detail, without failing to appreciate properly the extent and effective exuberance of purpose, the creation of God? I do not mean only the sky, the warmth of the sun, the immensity of the waters, the sumptuous grandeur of the plains, valleys and mountains, the whiteness of the snow, the almost unforgettable fragrance of the flowers, but also the tender and penetrating sense of the earth's beauty. To the tender and penetrating sense of the song of the birds, to the silent murmur of the rivers, of the waterfalls, to being able, perhaps, to be like a mother, as there are so many, who stop sleeping in the early hours to watch and contemplate the sighs of their children while they sleep. It would be a great ignorance to think that God, in creating, had in Himself a plan of enrichment. Creation was not a compliment to the divine ego, God did not create anything or anyone to satisfy himself, creation is the indelible and unfathomable sign that God created us not because he needed us to be a greater God, but God created us to manifest the explosion of the powerful force of his unbreakable essence. God beheld in creation a great beauty and saw in it a splendorous and eternal efficacy. God is love and everything we see, everything we touch, everything we feel, everything we smell and everything we taste, is a sensitive part of an explosion of love. When love explodes, it expands unbreakable and indelible particles that are God's own creative action. That is why I am not concerned about whether some will call this movement a chemical explosion, an explosion of atoms, or the **"Big Bang"**. *The name, it is the least important thing for this expression of natural or supernatural phenomenology, however you want to call it, is a dynamic movement, ultra mega powerfully incontestable in the universe, which takes place metaphysical transformation governing all aspects and in all and any extension that needs explicitly of force, of impulse not found in itself, but is only found fully and potentially in the creative grace of God.* (In Book VIII of the Physics, Aristotle speaks of a being as a pure immaterial act which undergoes no change and which is the physical principle of the world. Because he is not material, he himself is not something physical. Physics, II, 7, 198-36). Later, in Book XII (Lambda) of the Metaphysics, Aristotle argues for the existence of a divine being and seems to identify it with the "first immobile motor", perhaps influenced by the *Nous, Greek word* meaning: *full and unequivocal wisdom in no circumstance.* The prime mover cannot have magnitude, either finite or infinite and, consequently, it is indivisible and without parts. He defines it as an immobile and incorruptible substance as opposed to the sensible physical substances. This, coupled with the fact that in the ninth chapter he speaks of God, the life of the immobile motor is the self contemplative thought ("νοήσεως νόησις) *Noeseos Noesis, Greek word* meaning: *thought of thought*, because thought is superior and capable. According to Aristotle's philosophy, the gods cannot potentially be distracted from this eternal self-contemplation because, at that instant, they would cease to exist. This has led many authors to speak of Providence. Life also belongs to God; for the actuality of thought is life and God is that reality and the self-dependent actuality of God is the supremely good and eternal life. *Therefore we say that God is a living, eternal, supremely good being; so that life and duration belong continuously and eternally to God, because this is God. Metaphysics, 1072.*

God is the prime mover, God is the prime mover, God is energy, not an energy or part of some energy, God is the alpha and the omega, the manifesting principle of all other actions that were consecutive. It was not up to God to improve, but to establish the first principle so that all things, starting from Him, could find their fullness of existence. For God created everything without essentially removing His distance from the independence of free will, of allowing His creation to develop in itself the person of its existence from the creative principle. That is why the most remarkable sages, philosophers, theologians and other scientists, contemplating nature, were able to exploit the most beautiful experiences and researches updated in their knowledge. All that we call them: of luminous ideas, poems, compositions, arts, drawings, theses and compilations; everything they said, however relevant it may be, they have not managed to squeeze out the splendorous effect of the explosion of God's love, they have always left a gap of something that cannot be fully addressed in its maximum extent of depth and response. Even the most spiritually sensitive, inspired by divine beauty in creating their works, considered the most brilliant, have not yet been able to reach the precise splendor and grandeur of the explosion of God's creative love. When I speak of explosion, never understand that God is divided into particles, because God *is broken, but never divided*, this expression designates the action of the breaking of the bread that appears twice in the New Testament (Luke 24:35 and Acts 2:42). In every tiny part of this explosion of love, his omnipotence, his omnipresence and omniscience were and still are fully and totally present. God divides himself, but he does not divide himself and that perhaps, and I am sure of it, is the most relevant part of the secret of his love. God is unique, full and unrepeatable in each of his actions and in each of his works in the mystery of Father Creator, which consists in his first attribute, that is, that your communion with God is so important that, when you feel him, when you experience him, you do not do it in a partial or divided way, but you experience him in a full and real way, in his totality. He is truly God Emmanuel, God with us, God fully alive, real, efficacious, true and unbreakable. I invite you now to close your eyes and take a deep breath so that you can enjoy the experience you are having right now. That experience of God is the magnificent greatness of God himself, as he himself is and presents himself directly to you at this moment. Some people always ask me: *"Have you been able to see the face of God?"* My answer is always the same, *"It is something impossible to the limits of our human vision, grace itself allows us to enter into a profound mystery of love, from presence to presence, where the natural signs and dimensions, regularly recognized by human intelligence, cease to operate and give space to the power of mystical force"*. It is to enter into the dimension of the immeasurably beautiful love that can extend to the deepest part of your being and that you can call *ABBA*, which means Father. My almighty Father, I adore you, I praise you Lord, I bless you Lord because you are the only one who can permeate my entire being. You are my beloved Father, my creator, the one who endowed me with unfathomable graces, the one who gave me from heaven your image and likeness, blessed are you. Many children cannot call their fathers as fathers, because they were abandoned, in other cases very mistreated, abused, were victims of absent fathers or abusive fathers with their mothers at home, adulterous fathers, addicts, who left deep traces of frustration and shame in their children. I understand that for you it is very hard to discover or wish to seek any other type of fatherhood. That is why, for some, admitting the fatherhood of God is completely misguided. To your heart I would like to reach out now, to reveal to you that human fatherhood, however good and healthy it may be, still remains very limited and far removed from the potential and sublime divine fatherhood. As good as a father may be at nurturing his children, much more does the heavenly father know about us. He alone sheds unfathomable treasures and He alone can make up for every absence, lack, weakness and failure of this existence we live. *"If you then, being evil, know how to give good gifts to your children, how much more will your heavenly Father give the Holy Spirit to those who ask him?" (Luke 11:13).*

Why should I wish to resemble so many fashions and idols of misery if I can now, Lord, be born again, receive your Holy Spirit, receive the ineffable gift that comes from heaven, the forgiveness of my faults, of my sins, be washed, Lord, in your purifying waters.

"Come Lord and revive my heart, come Lord and rescue my life from death. Until today I have been a person of lesser worth Lord, I have felt incapable, unimportant, defeated, accused by many people, but none of that, Lord, can win over the powerful force of your image and likeness. Come Lord, you can reign, reign Jesus, reign Lord, with the power of creation in me, allow me to be born again, forgive me Lord, give me strength to overcome all prejudices, may these slanders and accusations be removed from me, oh mighty and blessed God! Come to the aid of my heart and tear out, Lord, this heart of stone to give me a new heart of flesh, sensitive and capable of beating and vibrating with the joy that comes from your most holy presence". (prayer of Surrender).

It is in this way that you will enter into the process of the new birth, to be born again is to recognize that only God can give you the necessary strength that you have sought to live with dignity, wisdom and justice. Truly, in all these years that I have helped so many people, with each one of them I have walked the path of this restoration towards new life. I have invited each one of them to the opportunity to go inside themselves and thus to be able to recognize that clearly, the secret directed towards them, many people reach it quickly, others take longer because of the difficulty they bring to open themselves to God and letting themselves be healed by the strength of his love. But something that brings me great security of faith is to know that at some moment God will reveal it splendidly and will make true rivers of living water gush forth from within me.

One day, many years ago, I had my encounter with God and it was on the mountain of despair, when I already judged that God had forgotten me, when I felt alone, abandoned not by God, but by those people that I was looking for assuming that they were very important in my life and it was there that Jesus appeared to me, and with great love and compassion, he extended his love to me, saying: *"I made you brothers, members of one another, but the head of your soul is always me, your hand will be able to help you, your feet will be very important, each one of your brothers are part of your life, but I am the brain"*. Jesus emphasized and spoke to me in different ways, repeating this teaching several times and in different moments and circumstances. This word became a lifetime goal and he repeated it to me saying: *"Learn, give yourself the opportunity to live with everyone, to love everyone, to cherish everyone as you cherish yourself, but do not forget to love me above all things".*

I remember that in my first great encounter with the Lord, in March, Holy Week 1986, in a youth retreat, I realized that I had a special calling and I realized that it would not be easy to endure all the challenges with faith and willingness. The moment I heard the voice of the Lord, I fell to the ground crying and all I saw were the feet of Jesus before my eyes. I had an experience similar to the sinner who entered Simon's house and washed Jesus' feet with her tears. Through my tears of sorrow, I saw all my history up to that day pass before me and I could see, by God's grace, what lay ahead, including my mistakes and great falls. The feet of Jesus became like mirrors, because I saw my whole life reflected in them, there were tears and tears that flowed when I felt that Jesus put his hands on my shoulders, he pressed me with an immeasurable love. He truly held me, as no one in my entire life had ever held me before, not even my parents and the people closest to me. I felt that the hand of Jesus permeated every part of my body up to my soul. I felt an immense warmth, a warmth of compassion, of forgiveness, of mercy, and the only thing I said to him was: "There is no turning back, I do not want to lose the touch of those hands". It was the experience of Tabor, I perceived that I was in another dimension, in another atmosphere, definitely, I was being born again, just as the doctor grasps in the air, with his strong hands, the baby that is born and jumps from his mother, at that moment Jesus was receiving a new child. A Rodrigo was being buried, destined to disgrace because of the conduct of the world, and at the same instant, by the mystery of God's love, another Rodrigo was being born, now a new man, saved, consecrated, anointed and marked to be a blessing for many that God, in His time, after forming me, would send them.

Now that you have heard my testimony, enter into prayer with me and ask for the possibility and grace of this encounter. Say to Him: *Jesus, may Jesus do the same in my life, I want to be born again, I want a new creation, a new vessel, break my heart, undo my illusions, break my chains, break the barriers, I want to be born of water and of the spirit, of your power, by the strength of the Holy Spirit. I need and want to be a new person, to have a new family, to reach the benefits of a new conduct, to be able to make new choices, to be able to leave aside stubbornness, indifference, laziness, to then, beloved Jesus, really enter into the sensitivity of spiritual things, to learn with sobriety and sincerity, to love the Holy Communion, your body and blood, to enjoy prayer in the silence of my house to adore you Lord, in spirit and in truth, to overcome my flesh thirsty of so much filth and perversity. I thank you, Jesus, for allowing me to make this decision, which I am convinced is the most authentic of all my life, I want to leave here my ignominy until today and enlist me among the number of your servants, bathe me in the water of the spirit, I love you eternally. Blessed be Thou and praised be Thou forever. Amen.*

Now that you have assumed with faith the purpose of beginning a new life, it is very necessary for you to understand that not only human beings and not only some privileged or some others, the most intelligent, can live and verify the exuberant greatness of God's benevolence. This grace embraces everyone, those who arrived at the *first hour* and those who arrived *at the end of the task.* **(Matthew 20:1-16)**; we can all enjoy this powerful encounter and adore the Lord with our whole being, receiving our inheritance in full.

The apostle St. John in Revelation 4:11 tells us: **"You are worthy Lord, our God, to receive glory, honor and power, because Christ, all things and by your high will, is that all things exist and were created in the holy mass, in the universal praise, each priest praises God saying:** "It is worthy and just to praise you, O Lord, for you are worthy to receive glory, honor and power: It is worthy and just to praise and bless you, to glorify and thank you, to adore you in every time and place because you are a God of real power, inscrutable to our reasoning, but always eternally existing, the same your only begotten son and the Holy Spirit; you from non-existence brought us into existence and after sin you raised us up again and accomplished exactly everything to bring us back to heaven offering us the future heavenly kingdom. For all these graces we thank your son Jesus Christ and the Holy Spirit, we thank all your benefits, those we knew and those that are still unknown to us, those revealed and those not revealed, we thank you for being present, celebration through the office of our hands we understood Lord, that thousands of archangels and angels, cherubim and seraphim with six wings and multiple eyes, fly before your eternal presence in the heavenly heights".

Our praise is not an obligation of our being before God, true and humble praise is born simply from the constant care of God's mercy that comes to each one of us so effectively and is renewed every morning. That is to say, friendship with God and the humble nearness of his presence, breaks our hearts and enables us to achieve gratitude and the desire to seek him through the prayer of praise. It is born from within us as a serene act of love. King David proclaimed: *"Bless the Lord, O my soul, and forget not all his benefits; it is he who forgives our iniquities and heals all our wounds mightily; it is he who rescues from death and restores life and crowns with his mercy and graces; it is he who satisfies us with good things and renews our existence, as the eagle renews his youth; the Lord is compassionate and merciful, patient and infinitely gracious; he will not depart forever, nor are his demands perpetual"* **(Psalm 102-109)**. The greatest and imponderable act of our inner self is to contemplate God's loving mercy towards us, to be able to understand clearly that he did not make us for misfortune and failure, but to be bearers of his immense love. By sending us his son Jesus Christ through the incarnation in the womb of Mary most holy, he manifested to the whole of humanity his unbroken desire to rescue us from the rebellious insolence that by sin we were trapped and enslaved. God the Father manifested through the incarnation of his only begotten son, his plan to rescue us from death and transport us definitively to the new birth through the passion, death and resurrection of our Lord Jesus Christ.

Sin is not just a whim or an isolated act of human ignorance, nor is it simple disobedience, sin is a direct rebellion against God's authority in our lives. Sin begins in the mind, migrates to the heart, deceives the senses and finally enslaves the actions.

During our last reflection we said that Christ's words in the Sermon on the Mount refer directly to the **desire** that is immediately born in the human heart; indirectly, however, these words guide us to understand a truth about man, which is of universal importance.

This truth about historical man, of universal importance, toward which the words of Christ taken from Matthew 5:27-28 direct us, seems to be expressed in the biblical doctrine of the threefold concupiscence. We refer here to the concise formula of the *First Letter of St. John 2:16-17: "All that is in the world, the lust of the flesh, the lust of the eyes, and the pride of life, is not of the Father, but is of the world. And the world is passing away, and so are its lusts; but he who does the will of God abides forever."* It is obvious that in order to understand these words, one must take into account the context in which they are inserted, that is, the context of the whole "theology of St. John", about which so much has been written. However, the same words are inserted, at the same time, in the context of the entire Bible; they belong to the whole of the revealed truth about man and are important for the theology of the body. They do not explain concupiscence itself in its threefold form, because they seem to presuppose that *the concupiscence of the body, the concupiscence of the eyes and the pride of life* are, in any case, a clear and known concept. Instead, they explain the genesis of the threefold concupiscence by indicating its origin, **not from the Father, but from the world.**

The concupiscence of the flesh and, together with it, the concupiscence of the eyes and the pride of life, is in the world and, at the same time, comes from the world, not as fruit of the mystery of creation, but as fruit of the tree of the knowledge of good and evil (Genesis 2:17) *in the heart of man.* What bears fruit in the triple concupiscence is not the *world created by God for man, whose fundamental goodness we have read more than once in Genesis 1: "God saw that it was good... it was very good".*

Instead, in the triple concupiscence fructifies the **rupture** of the first Covenant with the Creator, with God-Elohim, with God-Yahweh. This covenant was broken in the heart of man. **It would be necessary here to make a careful analysis of the events described in Genesis 3:1-6. However, I refer only in general to the mystery of sin**, at the beginning of human history. Indeed, it is only as a consequence of sin, as the fruit of the breaking of the covenant with God in the human heart, in the depths of man, that the *world of the Book of Genesis became the world of the words of St. John 1:2, 15-16: the place and source of concupiscence.*

Thus, the formula according to which *concupiscence does not come from the Father but from the world, seems to be directed once again towards the biblical principle.* The genesis of the threefold concupiscence, presented by John, finds in this principle its first and fundamental elucidation, an explanation that is essential for the understanding of what we will call: the theology of the body.

To understand that truth of universal importance about the historical man, contained in the words of Christ during the Sermon on the Mount (Matthew 5:27-28), we must return once more to the book of Genesis, pausing once more at the threshold of the revelation of the historical man. This is all the more necessary since this threshold of salvation history is, at the same time, the threshold of authentic human experiences, as we will see in the following texts.

On the ground of the Sermon on the Mount, according to St. Matthew, and precisely from the affirmation of Christ taken from *Matthew 5:27-28, "You have heard that it was said, 'You shall not commit adultery,' but I say to you that everyone who looks at a woman and lusts after her has already committed adultery with her in his heart".* Precisely by virtue of this truth, we try to grasp to the core the man that Christ indicates in the text of *Matthew 5, 27-28*; that is, the man who *looks at the woman desiring her*. In short, is this gaze not explained by the fact that the man is precisely a man of desire, in the sense of the first letter of St. John, and furthermore, that both, that is, the man who looks at the woman who is the object of this gaze, are in the dimension of the triple concupiscence, which does not come from the Father, but from the world? It is necessary, then, to understand what this biblical *man of desire* is, in order to discover the depth of Christ's words according to *Matthew 5:27-28* and to explain the meaning of his reference, so important for the theology of the body, to the *human heart*.

Let us return again to the biblical account of creation, in which the human race appears at first as a man of original innocence, **before original sin**, and then as one who has lost this innocence, breaking the original covenant with his Creator.

It is worth noting that the biblical description itself seems to highlight especially the key moment in man's heart when he questioned the gift of God's perennial grace. *The man who takes the fruit of the tree of the knowledge of good and evil makes, at the same time, a fundamental choice and makes it against the will of the Creator, God Yahweh, accepting the motivation suggested to him by the tempter: "No, you will not die; for God knows that on the day you eat of it, your eyes will be opened and you will be like God, knowing good and evil"; according to ancient translations: "You will be like gods, knowing good and evil".* This motivation clearly contains the questioning of the gift and love of those who understand the origin of creation as an effective gift of God.

It is enough to read carefully the whole passage of Genesis 3, 1-5, to determine there the mystery of man who turns his back on the Father by questioning, in his heart, the deepest meaning of the gift, that is, love as the specific motive of creation and of the original covenant (**cf. especially Genesis 3, 5**), *man turns his back on God-Love, on the Father.* In a certain sense he rejects him from his heart and as if he were cutting him off from that which **comes from the Father; thus what comes from the world remains in him.** *Man denies his direct origin from the image and likeness of God as a precious gift, in order to secure himself in the gift of the world, to secure himself in the promises of the devil, of the spirit of deception and perversity, of enmity and slavery.*

"Then they opened the eyes of both of them, and when they saw that they were naked, they sewed fig leaves together and made themselves girdles" (**Genesis 3:7**). This is the first sentence in the biblical account that refers to *man's situation after sin and shows the new state of human nature.* Does this sentence not also suggest the beginning of concupiscence in man's heart? In order to give a deeper answer to this question, we cannot stop at that first sentence, but we need to read the whole text again. **Genesis 2, 25 underlines that they were naked... without being ashamed of it,** already Genesis 3, 6 speaks explicitly of the birth of shame in connection with sin. *That shame is as the first source of manifesting itself in man in both male and female, which does not come from the Father, but from the world.* that is why sin is considered a disordered and uncoordinated action that engenders in man created *in the image and likeness* of God. Shame is the mark that expresses, from the most intimate part of creation, the original presence of sin.

The confusion and forgetfulness of who he really is and for what he was created, made the human being cling to sin. In itself, this is the rebellion of our own essence of man and woman created in the image and likeness of God for the glory, contemplation and existence in his love, that through weakness we have preferred to live according to the gift of the world, moving away from our own primordial origin, denying God and his love. Would it be much easier for God, after the realization of sin, to have destroyed men as corrupt, unworthy of his love? *The mercy of God from the first moment of the first transgression, began to lead sweetly and patiently the new step of humanity towards redemption through spiritual renewal.*

Mankind is invited, by God's grace, to understand that nothing in life happens overnight. *God works with us through a process of renewal, through a re-education of understanding, through the renewal of our behavior, of our spirit*, which will never be aggressive or manipulative, because He respects the particular and individual stage of each one of us. For God, time *(Kronos)* is not the most important thing, but the effects of time through grace *(Kairos)* in the natural and supernatural process of its re-education towards the new birth.

Being born again is not an imposed action of God but a sensible possibility that the Holy Spirit invites every human being so that he can return to the essential synthesis of his own existence; so that he can return to the essential origin for which he was created, to be the *image and likeness* of God. Is it possible for you to understand the power of all this? *Normally, when we are invited to a great feast or commemoration or even to a simple event, it is very important to take into account the dignity of the one who invited us, especially if it is something that gives us a place of prominence.* By God's grace we were invited, through creation, to participate in the unfathomable beauty of God reflected in it, God invited the human race to rule and dominate all his creation. *You were created from the existence of God and that must be for you cause and reason for great honor and great value and to know that you have the image and likeness of Him and that your creator makes you full heir of all the benefits that come from the one who inherited you, your great father, He, who is in heaven. Raise your head, lift up your gaze, clear your eyes, regain the sense of your feet, straighten your steps, strengthen your running footsteps, dignify the efforts of your hands, take hold of the efficacy by which God first honored you, in spite of all your sins, He mercifully wanted to forgive you.*

The essence of the great redemptive deed, performed by Jesus, is clearly explained in all the sacred texts that we find in the New Testament in the series of parables of the Gospels, such as the Gospel of the lost sheep and the lost drachma, of the prodigal son, the Gospel of the barren fig tree, the Gospel of the Good Shepherd, the Gospel of the Good Samaritan, of the workers in the vineyard and in so many others. It is easy to perceive when we are reading these sacred scriptures that humanity was lost as the sheep was lost, as the sheep that easily let itself be carried away by the attraction of shortcuts, or perhaps, was lost because it realized that it could not accompany the flock in the demands of faith, perhaps because of its high level of inner sickness and the prejudice of wanting to be strong and not share its real needs with others, or perhaps even, was lost because at some point it lost sight of the shepherd for having been dumbfounded and absent-minded in other charms. In the gospel of the **good shepherd**, the most striking thing is to observe the level of difficulty the shepherd had in finding and rescuing the lost sheep. The sacred text says that he searched through **mountains and deserts**. When someone is lost, is lost- very lost. We are hardly able to understand. Many do not understand their own relatives, spouses reject each other, accuse each other and obviously, out of great ignorance of the truth that they are going through, mistreat each other. Few truly understand how much pain and anguish it takes for a person to lose their ideals and their own life. Parents reject their children, denigrate them further with bad corrections. Friends are known to pull away and judge each other and most of the time, we make the person lose themselves even more, we close them off from the possibilities of changing their path to the proper and right path.

I want to share with you the story of Taylor, a 17-year-old young man I was able to help. He had had his upbringing in an irregular family due to many factors, vicious and abusive parents. At 15 he started using drugs and at 17 he was selling and dealing cocaine in the neighborhood. He truly hit rock bottom, until we met through his grandmother. After breaking the ice of fears, he told me: *"why change, no one trusts me, my family, only my grandmother"*. He could not find the impetus to return to the **new path** of life, because the very contempt and disinterest of his family did not serve as a ladder for him to get out of the bottom of the abyss. Perhaps in his family, or among his friends, there is a person going through the same thing and he needs a touch from heaven through someone to recover all that he lost and return to the flock of Christ. We need to fight as hard as we can to save our neighbor, no matter the price we have to pay, but we cannot let our loved ones sink deeper and deeper into the mess of the lost path. For many, perdition was the only likely path, precisely because of the absence of love and vibrant challenges for change.

Getting lost on the road is far from being just a physical loss, getting lost means disfiguring oneself from the initial plan of the route. A person can be in the same physical, territorial or material place as other people, but be totally lost in mind, intellect or affective location. He may still continue to have the same interpersonal and social contacts and relationships, but if his soul is lost within, the effects of the loss are severe and risky. There is something inside that does not allow full connection with himself and with the living and dynamic universe around him, something that is dragging the person to the wasteland, to a deserted place of abstraction. These conditions always refer us to the place of danger. This is the atmosphere that many of our young people are experiencing and that is why they are suffering so much, mostly in loneliness, because the people closest to them fail to understand this process and end up doing more harm instead of properly helping them overcome their inner challenges. Many are isolated in the world of technology, others in the world of the wrong direction of the perversity of values and others still locked in their rooms, in their homes, with a real phobia of life and people. Many are being treated as maniacs, schizophrenics, mentally ill, but in reality what they need is just someone to listen to them and share with them the gift of life.

Throughout my ministerial life as a priest and as a pastor of souls, countless times I had the experience of meeting people in these conditions of profound loss of values and of life itself; men, women, young people who were totally lost in themselves and their closest references. After listening to each of these people and realizing their desperate situation, it was not difficult to evaluate in each of them the aggressive consequences they were facing. For the pastor, spiritual director or counselor, it is not simply realizing that the **sheep**, the person we are trying to help, is in danger, but more than anything else, it is really understanding what kind of danger they are in. It's not just knowing that they are among thorns on the rock of perdition but being able to strategically identify how poisonous and hurtful these thorns are and how definitely destructive the abyss may be that this person is so vulnerable of falling into. Yet, when the shepherd finds the sheep that was lost and sees her almost dying, it is not just treating her wounds, but discovering the most effective means to make her understand that she needs to return to the flock, that being part of the flock is an essential reality of her identity as a sheep. The one who treats the wounded person needs to help her to understand the reasons for her painful wounds and together, to find means of resistance to all that is recurrent and hurtful. It is our challenge to bring her to understand what were the doubts and delusions that made her turn away from the main path of her life. Perhaps she left and got lost exactly because she did not feel loved, because she did not feel identified with anything around her, perhaps because she did not see herself in the condition to be in the front ranks near the pastor or perhaps because of her own situations and inner prejudices as a person.

Once in my life I had the opportunity to spend a few days on a farm where there was a large sheep farm and I asked the shepherd:

—*How do you go about creating closeness with your sheep?*

—*Oh, it's very easy, at the moment of shearing,"* he assured me.

I, half astonished, asked him how this happens. He kindly told me:

—*Looking at the herd, they are all white, beige, some brown and some black, but when I bring them individually to my arms and with the machine I start to shear them, I discover the true color of the skin that each one of them has. I find the spots on the skin, look more closely at their wounds, if they have parasites or other diseases. I dedicate quality time to them, then, immediately I realize what their particular needs are, even those with wounds on their paws or deformities. In that moment nothing is hidden from me, some of them I cannot subject to the long pastures that we usually take the others to, and some of them I realize that I need to keep them well kept for a while until they recover. Some of them, in spite of having very fluffy and long wool, when I shear them I find them fragile and very thin, so I understand that they need special nutrition.*

I had taken a few days to rest on that farm and God had led me to a deep time of learning to improve my service to my flock. To get to know my sheep, intimately, in the light of faith and truth, to better understand their lives and their real needs.

You cannot imagine what kind of class I took that morning, I understood that I was being taught practical theology, how to truly act as a flock shepherd and I began to imagine the many spiritual sheep of my flock in Long Beach, California and that is when Jesus told me once again: "You have to learn to shear your sheep so that you can learn to know the hidden identity of each one of them". God was inviting me to surrender even more, to seek to know in depth what He had entrusted me with.

But it is so difficult. It is an arduous path and very hard to take on. **Shearing means stripping.** For a while the shepherd's flock will go through the experience of losing its wool coat, it will lose the implantation of its external majesty, of that which in a very dense way ended up hiding the reality of each one of its sheep. This is how I realized that there are many sheep that, in spite of having very long wool and multiple hidden wounds, still resist to be shorn so that they can continue to cover their wounds and not be really known by the shepherd. It is the syndrome of the **necessary sickness** of those sheep that prefer to die sick and isolated than to discover and face what they really bring and are their real problems, because they are so afraid of not bearing the treatment and because they believe more in rejection and judgment than in the abundant mercy of God.

My dear children, Jesus is willing to carry you on His shoulders because you are His beloved sheep, because you are the fig tree that He wants to see blossom, because you are the person He created in His image and likeness. He is willing to give a thousand kingdoms or as many as it takes for you. You cannot imagine the great value you hold for Him; do not imagine God's desire to see you reach the fullness of your spiritual rehabilitation through the mystery of the cross of Christ. The Lord is waiting for you to understand the potential of redeeming love to save you from all the evils of sin. In spite of our transgressions, Christ agreed to die for us without sparing a drop of his most precious blood. I am sure and convinced that throughout your life, more than once you have done the mathematics of skimping, asking yourself: What could I do so my efforts are less? How could I do things so that sacrifice and hardship never reach my home? Or then, *how could you lead a life in the shadows, so that no one would see you, no one would question you, no one would mess with you?* Whoever skimps on living through challenges never discovers the power of divine providence, never discovers the caring hand of the shepherd, never experiences the true power of victory. However, when one decides to be completely healed, puts oneself on the altar of God, submits to be truly shorn, opens oneself to the process of liberation and inner healing, to the renunciation of lies, of false behaviors and friendships and with submission of faith allows oneself to be shorn, one is assuming with all one's heart that one desires to be a new person, a sheep cleansed from evil. In front of everyone he endures all the difficulties until he can compose himself again, so that when the new winter of difficulties arrives, he will find himself with sufficient strength, with a new garment of the grace of God, with new knowledge and intelligence truly renewed by the hands of our Lord Jesus Christ.

All that we are talking about is to awaken your life to the need for the healing of your personality. We need a healed Church and for that we need to be people willing to inner healing, not only to attend and attend spiritual services, but to be transformed by the grace of God into people taken by the spirit of God. Remember that every part of your story is being written, not only by your hands, but there are many notes, articles, concepts, that are being added over the years by the closest people, friends, companions along the way, but all of that is staying there, in the summary of a *supposed personality* that you believe to be yours.

What I really want is to bring you to understand about the powerful and profoundly capable force of God's love to touch the deepest and most original part of your particular personality. *God, through his healing love, wants and has the power to reach and permeate the most sensitive area that makes you believe that it is your person, that it is your being, that it is essentially the leading factor in your conceptions, apprehensions and actions.* Don't be so convinced that all of that, beyond the interior, is perfectly correct and regular. By the way, there are many things in disorder or causing disorder within you. All the interferences that were being made throughout your life, through the many different experiences and friends, caused within you many misrepresentations, confusions. Perhaps some concepts about you, formed by others, made you assume certain mistakes in your own personality. Definitely, everything that is not found with its origin in true love, the one that comes from God, can easily be transformed into deformation and possible fraud against your own personality. This is born from lies, slander, fabricated situations, by true deceivers and instruments of falsehood that approach lives in order to hurt and damage them. People who came into your life to bring torment, who only wanted to write in your life summary to confuse you, to make you believe things that you never really were, never did, never had, but your own cowardice and your fear to face, all these people made you let them manipulate your life project and the authentic formation of your personality.

During all these years of spiritual life, how many people I have met with damaged *life summary* and I had to, with the strength of faith, with the authority of pastor of souls and with classified prayer, help many people to erase their personalities aggressively defrauded by other bad people prior to the arrival of Jesus in their lives. It was a task that God put me, as a pastor of souls, to be able to take to the interior of these souls and people, the love of Jesus towards them revealed so that they would be able to make the decision in God to destroy curses, vices, bad habits, by the power of prayer and the following of the word of God. All this with the only objective of, in its totality, rescuing these defrauded personalities and leading them by faith to a conscious personality of the image and likeness of God.

I remember Alizeth, a beloved sheep that I was able to help. After some meetings and dialogues, in tears she told me: "Definitely, after talking to you fo all these days, I don't know who I am anymore!" And this for her reflected something totally sad, she had realized that her whole life was a big lie, she even said: "You destroyed everything I thought my life had been for the last 25 years". It was then that we both held hands, looked at each other and I said, *"Alizeth, don't be shocked by what I'm about to tell you, you need to be born again"*. I stood up and extending my hands over her head, I began to pray only saying:

"Lord, here is your daughter Alizeth, they have written in her life, inside her, a history of lies, they have distanced her from your love and your presence. A history of lies starting with the story of her birth and her real parents. Because of this, Alizeth has become more and more lost every day until she reached the point where you find her today, so I ask you now Lord, manifest in Alizeth's life the same grace that you manifested in the life of Nicodemus, allow her to be born again by the power of the Holy Spirit".

At that moment she fell to the ground in repose in the Holy Spirit *(for those who are not familiar with this phenomenon, it is a healing grace when the person touched by God feels a lack of physical strength and is under the action and intervention of the power of God healing and liberating)*. Alizeth had fallen in front of me. I understood that this work was totally God's work and that she was receiving great redemption. Her body on the floor went into the fetal position, like a baby in the womb, she began to cry like a baby in its mother's womb. The prayer took about an hour and a half and at the end of the prayer, Alizeth, getting up, hugged me with great gratitude and told me: "Monsignor Rodrigo, everything became very clear to me, I could return to the first moments of my life, I returned to my mother's womb and I was able to discover things that I had never understood during my whole life". She immediately made the decision that she had received healed her personality. Five years passed and I met her again and now, this time she brought me her husband and the twin girls they had had, and hugging me she said: *"Thank you for helping me find myself as a person, I was able, through the blood of Christ, to heal my personality wounded by the lie and then be free to love and find a true love".*

With immense affection, full of faith and truth I tell you this, because when I met Alizeth, she was deeply confused, she had had two abortions and in the moment I met her, she was totally lost, living a deep disconnection with her personality. However, when she assumed the new birth by the power of the Holy Spirit, she also assumed the encounter with the Lord and she was able to discover who she really was, according to the heart of God.

The proposal offered is to bring you as close as possible to your personal consciousness, pushing you towards the life of overcoming and inner healing, of total restoration of the personality through the encounter with the unfathomable love of God. The most important thing about the reality of the grace of God, is to decisively touch his mercy, is to meet the one who can restore every stage of your personality. Only the grace of God can infuse in your heart the fullness of a love, capable of overcoming all self-esteem and prejudices, all the experiences of lovelessness, leading you to an integrated experience with a *light that does not go out*. Each person who decides to assume this encounter, discovers it in the blessing.

Do not be discouraged, do not despair, the process of a transformed personality is given from an intimacy of faith, it is by knowing Him, discovering Him, letting yourself be touched by Him, letting yourself be rid of the sheep, that the Lord all powerful will show you that He is the good shepherd, that He is the shepherd of shepherds and will be able to forge and bring to your life the excellence of the new birth.

Here is a beautiful testimony of surrender and encounter with God. I would like to present to you a beautiful poem from the pen of the great Spanish mystic Saint Teresa of Avila, one of the best teachers of the spiritual life of the Church. Her writings are a sure model in the ways of prayer and perfection.

Let nothing disturb you,
let nothing frighten you,
everything passes,
God does not move.

Patience
all things come to pass;
He who has God
lacks nothing;
God alone is enough.

Lift up your thoughts,
to heaven, ascend,
for nothing grieve,
let nothing disturb you.

Follow Jesus Christ
with a proud chest,
and, come what may,
let nothing frighten you.

Do you see the glory of the world?
It is vain glory;
it is nothing stable,
everything passes away.

Aspire to the celestial,
which always lasts;
faithful and rich in promise,
God does not move.

Love her as she deserves
immense goodness;
but there is no fine love
without patience.

Trust and lively faith
keep the soul,
for he who believes and hopes,
attains all things.

From hell beset
though it be seen,
shall mock his fury
he who has God.

He shall be in distress,
crosses, misfortunes;
God as his treasure,
he lacks nothing.

Go then, you worldly goods;
Go, vain joys,
even if you lose everything,
God alone is enough.

The great interest, if we can say so, of God's plan in the particular mystery of our existence, is to make the whole of humanity discover with such simplicity, that God is not concerned with what we do, but with what we are truly capable of discovering in the course of our existence, who we are within ourselves. With the boldness of love, the creator longs to see in his creation the fullness of his capacity to overcome failed acts, unnecessary ways and false attachments. He waits like a sentinel for the dawn, with a yearning for love, to meet our inner self, ready for a life superior to the everyday miseries. I am definitely convinced that for us, human beings, there is a great fear of facing the new. There is always a doubt that does not allow us to launch ourselves to discover something new. Perhaps the reason is because we carry in our history a very big load of falls, of incapacities, of badly resolved histories, of beginnings of so many things without being able to reach the end, of unfinished works, and this happens in the most diverse experiences of our daily life. We are afraid of what is new, as well as what is enormously attractive, the novelty of life in any circumstance, always puts us in front of the challenge to move towards what is different from what we are already accustomed to. It is impossible to embrace and all its demands, without being able to give up things from the past. Maintaining the two realities takes too much energy. To keep serving two masters causes a great imbalance in the scales of our existence, *"no one can serve two masters" (Luke 16:13).*

I would like to speak precisely to the generation of the 60s, the 70s and the 80s. From my generation, from the people I know who have gone through similar things and who still carry in our lives the desire, the deep longing, a search for the new, we still find the strength to move forward and to improve ourselves. However, I also find people of these generations who lost this desire to move forward and were defeated and trapped by little things and attachments, trying to keep the past, believing that there is nothing good in the new, retrograde people. People with a destructive and negative thinking, people who are locked in principles that no longer adapt to the family, to the children, to the way of relating to the novelty and expansion of the great discoveries.

I am not saying in accepting the absurd and perverted, but that these people may, by the grace of God, open and renew their understanding in order to be able to accompany with intelligence and in the light of the wisdom that comes from the high heavens, the movement that is happening around them and to be able to emit concepts adequate to the will of God and the welfare of themselves and their fellow men.

When we put everything we are seeing and living submissively, in line with the plan of the organization, we can understand that no decision can be taken before a real observation followed by authentic planning. Life cannot be lived inconsistently, parents, children, no one can live waiting every day for the next bomb to explode in the family, at work, at school, in life itself. That is living in the darkness of ignorance.

It is necessary to start thinking about our life in the light of faith, of God's grace and favor, to learn to plan our days according to God's goodness and generosity. The one who makes that decision discovers that life is not in one's hands, it is God who knows us and sustains us first, but also makes the decision of a foresighted and organized life, free of things that can put his days at risk. Clearly I am talking about prevention, this is the task of men and women. We take care of prevention and God takes care of providence. When these two things work together, we can overcome challenges and achieve success and blessing.

Some people I know, including parents, bishops and people with intellectual development with some advancement, believe that they are already outdated, defeated and spoiled. My questions are simple: *Who invented this lie, who wrote this note in the history of your personality, who was the one who tricked you into feeling you had no chance?* Only God has the ultimate power over your life. *"Not a leaf falls from the tree without the will of God" (Cervantes).*

When referring to the transformed personality, we are speaking directly to the personality at the core of our brain. The drawing and profile of someone's personality is there, but it is not static, it can be changed and transformed at any moment, Christ is the only one who has the power to perform such a miracle. *In many cases of people that I accompanied and still continue to help through spiritual direction, I could observe that some people present a personality profile that is tired, weakened, depressed, accustomed to the same and addicted to a number of fragile and lethal attachments.*

But if there is something wonderful in our personality, it is the capacity of our brain to transform itself, it is its capacity to be re-educated, the capacity to be able to experience and confirm actions, the capacity to achieve purification of realignment. This capacity will never be merely suggestive, it is the product of the educated will and of the conscious desire that is born from the autonomous decision of the personality, that is, from yourself, from your decision, from doing what Nicodemus did, listening to a new proposal to be **born again (John 3).** Many people look for me and almost all of them, without any difference, ask me: What can I do to change? I want to be different, I want to be a more active person, I want to be a more capable person, I want to look for new things, to seize new opportunities! What do I have to do?

My advice is to start working on your will power, get to know your likes and dislikes. This is the real stuff, the most sensible thing to evaluate the context of your existence. If you really want to work your will, you have to be willing to undress all the inner realities, be they positive or negative, in order to reach the most sensitive part of your will.

It is extremely necessary that someone accompanies you and helps you in this process of discovery. A good spiritual director willing to work under the guidance of the Holy Spirit, with hands of love, capable of touching with great charity the existence, each reality in your interior. It is not an easy task, nor is it to be done very quickly. To reach the will of a soul is to reach the spiritual DNA, and an unsuccessful act can cause serious consequences. Working the personal will of each one for a true healing and conversion to faith, demands that the whole character be placed on the altar of God by faith, so that you, freely and by your free will, can choose towards that which will truly change your existence totally. It is not enough just to say: *"I am going to think differently, I am going to love differently, I am going to assume to be a new person".* It is true that with your lips you confess your decision, but each one of us has a box inside our existence; we can call it *Pandora's box (a name originating from Greek mythology).* I do not know if you have ever been able to open your Pandora's box, which is the box where everyone keeps not only cravings. It also keeps the evils, the vices, the substrates of intrigues, hatred and grudges, the losses of unattainable things, frustrations and envy.

When you decide to open it you will have to be prepared to face your horrible inner shadows. *Once I was giving an inner healing retreat for some people in my community. I had known all the participants for a long time and I had been working with them on the inner healing of the will. I knew that this retreat would be decisive for the life of some of them. In the afternoon, after the talks, we began the prayer, I was praying sitting down, but powerfully, so that at that moment those dark boxes would be opened and the lives healed. There was a great cry of horror and I told everyone to keep their eyes closed. I knew that at that moment one person's box had been opened and all the dread was coming out, things that had been haunting them for years were being released. The person was crying and screaming very loudly, next to her was her husband, who was trying to stop her by closing the box, he was doing it perhaps because he was frightened by the human outrage that was produced in screams and coarse movements. But what had begun could not be stopped until all that was removed and the box was truly clean to receive the grace of the Holy Spirit. I drew near and continued to pray, until my eyes saw the magnificent power of God and the greatness of His mercy. I saw that woman being delivered, purified, redeemed and restored by the Holy Spirit, a miracle of God.*

If you want to transform your personality, if you want to transform your way of being, clean your inner self, you have to open the box you have inside, where the negative deposit that does not allow you to be fully free is. You have to learn to manage new treasures, now with excellent values, enriching your life and the universe around you. Choose those things that are really relevant for their value, importance, dignity, depth of concept, that really serve others. It is time to let out the good that is within you to infect humanity with light. We must make manifest the joy of God in our lives, our faith, our gifts and charisms, our inner beauty, which many times we ourselves hide and deprive others of enjoying and appreciating.

Why not start with the change capable of valuing all the good things in you. Even though I am a great sinner, despite my mistakes, my failures, every day I say to the Lord: *"My Lord help me, I have the need to experience this deep fire that you every day ignite within me, make me burn in your presence, consume me in your merciful love, forgive me, lift me up, help me to overcome my fears, to keep my life placed in your most holy presence, do not let me lose the desire to love and praise you, conquer me as many times as possible and necessary in order to stop me kept in your hands, as a little bird, protect me within your hands. I know, Lord, that you are setting my soul on fire, I know that you are training my interior with your signs and spiritual gifts, I know that you are moving my soul to be your servant at the service of my brothers, I am not worthy of so many favors, but I praise you for having chosen me as your instrument of love for the healing of hearts. I want to discover the value of each of your actions within me, I want to be able to appreciate the small details of your goodness and the great details of your generosity, I want to contemplate and experience what you do for me every day. I know that it is a unique work, that you, at that moment, are not repeating in anyone, your purposes for me are unique and I want to be faithful to each one of them. Amen."*

It is part of the process of liberation and healing, of your will to make the decision not to allow your soul to remain so bitter, to definitively block the development within you of a victimized soul, an interior abstracted from the grace of God. Deny the lazy will to remain with the thought controlled by a soul that makes you think that all you have, all you attract in your life, is misfortune, misery and oppression.

You must overcome and break with the forces that come from within you and reflect a selfish soul doomed to failure.

It is time, the grace of God invites us to receive the breath of wind that comes from the Holy Spirit and with boldness of faith, begin to classify the beautiful things that are potentially within us and around us, of the many details and favors of divine providence in our lives. It is time for inner cleansing, time to recognize and open the treasures within you, all of them generously deposited by God to bring you to the fullness of happiness. Give you the possibility to share with those who are closest to you, to those who are within your reach through the communication networks, their most excellent thoughts, which can truly enlighten and guide others towards the good of their lives as well.

It releases the capacity that was bound before, and now, by your decision to change the will, makes you able to discover part of a great gear that needs your strength to move life and direct everyone towards the good. We need to wake up, wake up our home, our children, our parents, our siblings, our friends, as many as possible. Life needs to be lived in an integral way and not just satisfying disordered impulses, there is much to build and great things we can assume if we change the purpose of our will.

To transform the personality is to give you the opportunity to contemplate the good that comes from you from the grace of God, it is to give you the opportunity to leave the dark and gloomy world of darkness to enter the world of light.

In the allegory of the cave, written by Plato, he describes the man who is at the bottom of the cave looking at the dark wall and only sees shadows reflected by a small light that enters through a crack. Tired of seeing shadows, he decides to turn around and face the light, to get out of foolish ideas and to go closer and closer to the real, until he touches the light of reality.

How many people have I met in the same condition, looking at the wall, believing they are seeing everything, but they are really trapped by shadows and distorted reflections. Staring at nothing or at things without understanding. It is necessary to give yourself the opportunity to face the light. *"Once again Jesus addressed the people and said to them, I am the light of the world. He who follows me will not walk in darkness but will have the light of life." (John 8:12).*

In the parable of the *Prodigal Son (Luke 15),* we perceive that he begins to come out of the dark wall when he allows himself to observe and evaluate the misery of his situation. His inner transformation begins when he realizes his profligate personality, his vices, his rebelliousness and disobedience to his father, the distance he was at from the dignity of his father's house. His will is awakened and he begins to remember the times of yesteryear, in his father's house, where those simpler employees ate better than he was eating at that moment. He was really going through the healing of the will.

Whenever I speak with young people, with parents and with people in general, I try to tell them and explain to them well that in their lives not everything has been a misfortune. *With immense love I invite them to the possibility of thinking that at some point in their lives they have had something wonderful, they have gone through something very beautiful, they have had the opportunity to experience something that one day made them strong and feel very loved, because we all have something of the parable of the prodigal son directly related to our lives.* At this point in the dialogue, the vast majority of people begin to cry and almost always I with them. It is wonderful to discover how good and great God has been to us and how much He can still do to awaken us to His love. *With propriety I lead them to understand that perhaps because of haste, eagerness, lack of commitment, the excesses of a soul without discipline and spiritual education, because of the disordered desire to have things without previous planning and due effort, they got into the wrong way.* Every soul shepherd must know how to lead his flock to this moment of restoration from the truth. It is the time to confront the soul with the liberating light of Christ. I know that this moment is painful, it causes discomfort, but once overcome, it produces a profound peace of renewal. The fruit of this spiritual ministry is to offer you the possibility to begin a process of re-assimilation and inner re-education, capable of making you leave misery and repentant of your disobedience, to return to the fellowship of God's abundance, being restored friendship, relationship and favors full of benefits.

As I want and desire to see you free and restored, may you enter with me into that garden of graces and miracles, may you at this moment pray with me and say: *"Lord, I want to be close to you, close to your love, close to your goodness, I need Lord, that my personality, which was darkened, which is now under the shadow of destruction, may reach the powerful force of light. I need Lord, that you give me the grace that my personality be healed, that my personality be re-educated, that all the cognitive levels of my being be touched so that they are enlightened and awakened to true life in God. I also ask Lord that you may tap the sensitive levels of my emotions and the spiritual levels. I seek you Lord, that I may attain the grace of your love to assume, through my healed will, the power of choice in your love, to gain a transformed personality at the touch of your unfathomable grace. I want to be taken by the force of a personality transformed by the power of repentance. Come Lord and bless me, blessed are you forever. Amen.*

Perhaps you think that this prayer is just a play on words, and with the same words I am trying to persuade him, but I can give you a beautiful example from the Bible, which is the change of the personality from Saul to Paul, it was not only the name that was changed, but also the character, the personality and the real way of conceiving things and situations. It was the change of the man who was once a great persecutor of the Jews, who after witnessing the martyrdom of St. Stephen, the one who was on his way to kill Christians in order to dispel the proclamation of the gospel. He definitely went through a very radical change of thought.

The change of inner and outer attitude of the violent vigilante, who by the force of his sword glimpsed the triumph of cleansing the east of the followers of Jesus.

On the road to Damascus, he hears the voice of Jesus, he sees the great light that powerfully blinds all the plans of violence and death that once fueled his decisions. The light hardly touches his legs, his feet, his hands, his inner health. It touches his whole and complete being, it embraces the most intimate part of his consciousness and personality to change from the depths. There was then a great commotion, a real encounter between rescuing grace and the sinner disoriented in evil (Acts 9). It was an encounter with the risen Lord *(Kyrios)*, which compelled Paul to adopt a new way of life; it was the experience that turned the Pharisee Saul into the apostle Paul. His character was touched, he felt the presence of the power of heaven, he recognized his condition and the error that dominated him. That legalistic personality, blind to the truth which made him act like an inconsequential criminal, is now immediately transformed by the sublime and perennial touch of the grace of God. The power of the healed and restored personality proper to the man of God is quickly reflected.

He heard :

—*Saul, Saul, why do you persecute me?*

—*Who are you, sir? —Saul asked.*

—*I am Jesus (of Nazareth), whom you are persecuting, —he was told.*

Paul himself wrote about this experience that God was pleased to reveal his son to him so that he might preach the good news about Jesus to the Gentiles (Galatians 1:15-16). It was an experience he never forgot, to which he frequently associated his apostolic mission. *"Am I not an apostle? Have I not seen Jesus our Lord?"* (1 Corinthians 9:1; 15:8).

This revelation of Jesus, the risen Lord, on the road to Damascus was to be the decisive factor that would henceforth dominate his whole life as an apostle among the Gentiles. For Christ's sake he became *all things to all men* (1 Corinthians 9:22). Consequently, from his encounter with the Lord and the change of personality, he became a *servant of Christ* (Galatians 1:10; Romans 1:1;), like the great servants of God in the Old Testament *(Moses - 2 Kings 18:12; Joshua - Judges 2:8; David - Psalms 78:70)*, and perhaps even like the Servant of Yahweh himself *(Isaiah 49:1; cf. Galatians 1:15)*.

It is from the encounter with the light that the human being confronts himself and realizes what he has been, perceives that all that he has lived has not led him to good things, then, he decides to let himself change. This decision to change is exactly to allow oneself to experience the direct interference of God's grace. Paul felt the inner impulse after his encounter with the light. Later Paul spoke referring to this experience, of the moment when he had been *taken up by Christ Jesus* (Philippians 3:12) and a kind of **necessity** impelled him to preach the gospel (1 Corinthians 9:15-18). He compared that experience to God's creation of light: *"For it is the God who said, 'Let light shine out of darkness,' who has shone in our hearts to give the light of the knowledge of the glory of God in the face of Christ"* (2 Corinthians 4-6). The impulse of God's grace urged him to work in the service of Christ; he could not *resist* against this sting (Acts 26:14). His response was that of a living faith, with which he confessed, together with the early church, that *Jesus is Lord* (1 Corinthians 12:12; Romans 10:9; Philippians 2:11). But this experience enlightened, in a creative act, Paul's mind and gave him an extraordinary insight into what he later called *"The Mystery of Christ"* (Ephesians 3:4).

This interference of grace is definitely greater than our capacity and our will. God takes us and moves us into the mystery of his love. God's impulse does not disorient us, the *sting* of grace places us in the focus of our mission as children of God called to mission. The *sting* burns, scorches and hurts in our being and allows us to understand that there is no rest as long as we do not do what has to be done. St. Augustine said: *"You made me Lord for you and my heart will be restless as long as I do not rest in you"*. Calm your heart, soothe your senses, let yourself be guided by this ineffable power of God.

The healed and adjusted personality, guided and enlightened by the grace of God, changes the course of our history. Healing the personality is the effective means that makes us settle down. A mature personality, confident of its potential, makes us put our feet where they belong and assume the benefits that are available to us as a result of our actions. I assume that you agree with what you are reading and really have access to this knowledge for the well being of your life. It may be that at this moment you are awakening inwardly and evaluating what you still lack to have a personality guided by the power of the light of God's grace, a personality unison to God's will, a personality disposed to grace.

Close your eyes and pray with me this instant. *Lord, how many things have done damage to my personality, words were spoken and above all heard, thoughts of mine and those introduced by a series of other means, wrong and cursed people who for a time forged my ideals, objects, circumstances, administrative systems, the political system itself, bad habits, their implications, concepts heard and admitted in an incorrect way. All that, Lord, has been completely working my character and personality, leading me to many errors. All that has forged in my character a set of actions that have made me, aggressively, show a selfish personality, an indifferent personality, an envious personality, a self-absorbed personality that does not allow me to see the needs of my fellow men, that does not allow me to get close to those closest to me. Perhaps, Lord, the only thing my personality wants is to see, at any cost, an individualistic personality that does not allow me to see your presence, that does not allow me to see the blessings you do for me every day. O mighty God, bless me, encamp around my existence your holy angels, they will be able to awaken me to all the progressive cares that you have for my soul. Blessed are you Lord for your light that shines before my eyes at this moment. I believe that the great tragedies I have lived through, the adversities I have faced, were not because you have punished me or sent that as a punishment to my life. I am sure that all that happened to me for wanting to maintain an irregular life, for maintaining an obsessed personality. For a long time I stopped experiencing, with use of reason, the sensitive and subtle signs of your protection. But at this moment, Jesus, I ask you not to let me continue to sink in this almost endless pit of selfishness, vanity and obsession, which blinds me more and more. Lord, grant me the good of healing my personality, help me Jesus to submit myself to the limits of justice, truth, faith, hope and love. Lord, where there are blockages that enslave my personality. Lord, may my whole being be enlightened by the grace that comes from you, that comes from your divine compassion. Blessed, praised, adored and glorified be you my Jesus.*

There is no way to heal the personality without strength, we must seek this strength in the Holy Spirit, in this powerful gift, capable of lifting up the weakest. St. Paul, in his first letter to (1Timothy 2, 4): *"I would that you had this awareness, God's desire is that all men be saved and come to the knowledge of the truth"*. To come to the knowledge of the truth is to reach the goal of obtaining a restored personality. No one can claim to know God if he still maintains a perverted, destroyed, corrupted and lying personality. The knowledge of God, this fire that burns within us, this heat that consumes us, this joy that dilates our souls, is really the effective symptom of a re-educated personality. Let us not stop believing in each other, let us not believe that you can say that a person will never change, that this person will never be a new person. To deny the possibility of change through healing is a great trap of the proud and perverse. It is obvious that all of creation, in all its aspects, can be changed and restored. The personality can be transformed, can be re-educated, can undergo a new birth by the grace of God. Blessed are those who believe, those who pursue this gift, those who experience, those who enjoy, those who live this power, because this power is not human power, nor is it a recurrent human decision, it is the direct and exclusive acceptance of God's grace.

I have found in the various communities that I have worked as a priest, many people who believe that temperament, character and personality are the same thing. Throughout time, different areas of science have been studying their differences. To know them is to open the door to a new threshold of knowledge and understanding about what leads to healing, our own and others, since not everything that manifests itself defines us and it is in the subtlety of being where the charm and personal characteristics lie.

Temperament is the raw material that serves as a pillar and base for the conformation of character and personality. According to specialists, it is innate, can have many inherited traits and is unmodifiable (which does not mean that it cannot be molded through practice). But that does not mean it cannot be healed by the power of grace, through the Holy Spirit's own gifts. I have known innumerable and countless people who suffered greatly because of their maladjusted temperament and who, by submitting their lives to spiritual teaching, were letting the violent temperament die out, making room for the new birth of a truly peaceful and peacemaking temperament.

The temperament has been classified into four types, based on an early assessment made by Hippocrates, a physician of ancient Greece, considered the father of medicine. Currently, his postulate is summarized in these four styles:

- **Sanguine temperament:** they are those cheerful, optimistic people, they like to be in company, they have warmth. Their way of acting favors feelings more than rational analysis. *They change their mind easily and find formal discipline difficult, since they privilege immediate pleasure.*
- **Phlegmatic temperament:** They are people prone to behave calm and serene, with perseverance and a certain rationality, to focus on their goals and objectives. *They value precision in thinking and doing. They tend to hide their*

anger and even hide their emotions, so they are sometimes seen as somewhat cold. They are often shy and avoid being the center of attention or holding leadership traits that expose them too much.

- **Choleric temperament:** They are energetic, proactive people, with a tendency to do and undertake. *Firm in their convictions, they trust in their own criteria and tend to confront others. They like to exercise positions of leadership and power. Sometimes they are inflexible, which leads them to polemicize or generate confrontations.*

- **Melancholic temperament:** They are sensitive, creative, perfectionist, persevering and somewhat introverted. *It is difficult for them to make decisions because of their tendency to want everything to go flawlessly and because of the insecurity of losing control of what is going to happen, they are easily crushed. They have a tendency to feel underlying sadness or melancholy.*

While we are born with temperament and it is the first referential of what we can potentially assume to be in life, *character is the result of the work of molding that first initial trait.* Thus, character is modifiable, educable, acquired and can be molded and controlled in its various external manifestations. Generally, the basis of character is formed in childhood and adolescence, within the home, with those closest to us. This education is given in a natural way by those responsible for the formation of the youngest. Many of us do not imagine the impact that children and adolescents can have based on us adults. They are forming their lives and from our teaching, they will form their character to be expressed in youth and adulthood, in front of all their actions through relationships, education, social interaction and experiences. *Can you imagine the dimension of their responsibility?*

I would like to open up your knowledge by teaching you about the different types of character we live with all the time.

- **The nervous character** (emotional, inactive, primary): Vividly feels stimuli and generates usually very strong emotional reactions. *It is hypersensitive. It has a high potential of energy that, as it does not discharge it conveniently, is seeking to come out as instincts or antisocial tendencies. Reacts almost immediately, without measuring consequences.*

- **Passionate character** (emotional, active, secondary): Nostalgic, bursts into jealousy or hatred. Predisposed to sacrifice; has a long-term vision and is accustomed to pay prices for what he/she wants. *Seeks to be compassionate and understanding. Good commanding ability and is a good leader. Great ability to work, although if given the choice, prefers to do it alone. Responsible and dedicated.*

- **Choleric Character** (emotional, active, primary): Bold to undertake new tasks, has emotional outbursts or outbreaks. *Extroverted and good with social relationships. Abandons goals in the face of difficulties; a bit scattered; has difficulty with discipline. Efficient at improvising, quick to respond. Generous and helpful; practicality.*
- **Sentimental Character** (emotional, inactive, secondary): Introverted and with few social skills, except with those with whom they really open up. Sensitive to the extreme. *Difficulty adapting to change; little flexibility. Conservative spirit. Logic and abstract thinking are often difficult. Strives to do things right. Easily demotivated; low self-confidence and this leads to sluggishness.*
- **Sanguine character** (non-emotional, active, primary): Extroversion at its highest level and practicality at its best. *Certain tendency to selfishness and greed. They are ironic and cynical; they use harsh criticism. Easily able to understand and reason objectively. Seeks quick results, even financially. Great self-confidence. Cold thinking.*
- **Phlegmatic character** (non-emotional, active, secondary): Coldness, which they use to hide their nerves and keep calm. *Constancy for their projects. They tend to be less expressive, autonomous and favor freedom. They adapt to changes. They show temperance; they have pride and tend to be orderly and methodical.*
- **Amorphous character** (non-emotional, inactive, primary): Lazy and accommodating to circumstances. They choose to be insensitive. Brave and docile behavior. *They seek to satisfy the senses, so they tend to eat, sleep or drink in excess. Slow in reasoning, they are carried away by the moment. Lives without showing worries. Disorderly.*
- **Apathetic character** (non-emotional, inactive, secondary): They are people who can be trusted. Certain tendency to live in the past and in learned habits. *Little vital enthusiasm; they do not like change. Low will and desire. Pessimistic attitude and maintain a routine because it gives them what they understand such as security, loneliness, melancholy.*

The integration of temperament and character determines the way we act, defined as personality, exactly where we are through this process, finding healing. The relationship with God can transform our temperament, sanctify our character and reveal to the world a renewed personality.

IV. Love and its Unconditional Power

"Love is patient, it is kind. Love is not envious or boastful or proud. It does not behave rudely, it is not selfish, it is not easily angered, it does not bear grudges. Love does not delight in evil but rejoices in the truth. It excuses all things, believes all things, hopes all things, endures all things."
(1 Corinthians 13:4-7).

"*Enlarge the space of our dwelling, he says. Intone the joyful or barren song, you who were not able to give birth. Exult with shouts of joy. Exult you who did not feel the pains of childbirth because more numerous are the children of the abandoned than the children of a wife, says the Lord Almighty. Lengthen and widen the spaces of your tent. Extend the curtains of your dwellings. Do not stop. Lengthen and make great your moorings. Strengthen your stakes, for you shall transship to the right hand and to the left. Your offspring shall take possession of other lands and repopulate forsaken cities. Do not fear for you shall not be ashamed. Do not be humiliated for you shall never be confounded. Indeed you shall forget the shameful condition of your past and remember no more the time of your forsaking, for your husband shall be the Almighty God, your creator, lord of hosts. He is a man and the holy one of Israel is your redeemer".* (Isaiah 54:1-5).

As we listen to the narrative of the beautiful passage revealed in the prophet Isaiah, it is quite certain that our hearts are immediately set ablaze and are promptly filled with a genuine desire to come out of abandonment and enter into direct contact with the work of love that comes from God.

Once, many years ago, I heard something in a spiritual retreat in the camp of God. The master of this retreat spoke to us about the mysterious tent, which was the Holy of Holies, the most holy place. The priest was inviting each one of us to be able to leave our personal tent and enter directly into this tent where the Lord Almighty was.

I distinctly remember that first night of the retreat I could not sleep. My inner self was not worthy to enter the most holy place. It was a night of many tears of repentance. At about two o'clock in the morning I realized that I had entered the room where a ***special visitation*** was. To this day I do not know if it was an angel or the living presence of Jesus himself. A powerful light came to visit me. It was a night of a rescuing encounter. In spite of my smallness and human misery, I was experiencing the promise of the visiting presence of grace in my distress. The ultimate truth of that night was that I felt and could clearly see that the small chamber I was in had been transformed into a sumptuous room filled with the divine presence, and I perceived that the grace of heaven had come to come to me and more precisely, to knock at the doors of the mysterious place that was my heart. God sent his grace to restore every weakness of low spiritual esteem. The impact was so great that the only thing I could think of doing was to fall with my face to the ground and prostrate not only my body, but all my exterior and interior senses. Celestial canticles were heard. Angels were singing. A beautiful praise in tongues was heard, and I could perceive that a great hand was approaching my head. At that hour I had no doubt, it was definitely God telling me: *"My son, my little Rodrigo, my little man that I want to make great, I want today to appreciate your vocation and the call that I gave you from your mother's womb. I need to open space in your heart so that you can love without fear or prejudice. I want to heal your cowardice. I want to free you from all the traps that prevent you from being what I have planned for you. I want to remove from you this condemnation that distresses you and give you back the powerful strength of trust in you and in grace. My child, I only need you to trust in my word, in every detail that I will teach you along your steps. Never take shortcuts. I am with you and I renew my covenant of love for you."*

At that instant, such a great fire entered my soul that I felt that everything in me burned and burned; I did not feel ashamed of my past. What filled my heart was an immense gratitude that only he who discovers the mysterious love of God, the love that is not an invention of the mind, not a madness or a hysterical and unbalanced ecstasy, can understand. My soul was serene and all my senses and mental faculties were under the reason of faith. My whole existence had been taken up into the love of God. Then one can understand the secret place, where one can touch and feel touched by the essence and potency of the Holy Trinity, exactly as it was at the moment of creation.

"Lord, how could I, my Lord, let myself be so deceived, hide behind idols and vices, how could I accept, Lord, for so long to have a personality far from you? Thank you Lord, because you have come to me. Thank you Lord, because you have called me by name. Thank you Lord, because in spite of your greatness and your power, you have decided, out of love, to seek me among the thorns of spiritual drowning and to offer me your mercy. You are the pilgrim of love, who is on pilgrimage at the doors of our homes, the only thing you want, Lord, is to enter and dwell among us".

I invite you to receive the visitation of the Lord. Only when you truly discover this immeasurable love of God, only when you go up with Jesus on the cross, when you surrender yourself to him and allow all your sins to be immersed in his most precious blood, will you have the strength to wait in the cenacle of faith for the powerful coming of the Holy Spirit.

Many people want to pray in tongues, to have the gifts of vision, of revelation, of healing, of knowledge, all this is possible. These are gifts poured out by the Holy Spirit for the edification and improvement of the Church. It is not for our own aggrandizement, but for the welfare and maintenance of the body of Christ, the community of faith. All this is very simple. It is a real and visible consequence of the attunement that each one of us develops with the Almighty God. When we truly meet Christ, the Lord enlarges the space of our dwelling place, widens it for all that was narrowed by selfishness and by our own vain pride. *His grace fills us with a profound illumination. The Lord establishes us in the word. He himself gives us a hunger for righteousness. He breaks our hearts. His healing freedom allows us to come out of the atmosphere of chained misery where everything is lost and relativized, in order to, with his generosity, introduce us to another level, another status and dwelling of faith.* The encounter with the Lord changes the curtains of our interior. Those curtains that before were traps contrary to the entrance of the light, deceptions for the distraction of the soul that did not allow us to look outside, are now transformed into glorious panels, in wide windows of hope, that allow us to see his glory, his power, to contemplate the light of the science of the Holy Spirit.

The grace of God works opening the interior towards the undoubted spiritual inspiration, awakening us to the vocation of kings, priests and prophets, grace received by the triple anointing in our baptism. This grace cannot remain paralyzed and stagnant in us. It must expand through our witness, which is our eloquent response to the call to proclaim the time of the *good news*, the gospel of Christ. The power of the Holy Spirit is enlarging in us his knowledge, through the gift of knowledge, wisdom, counsel, fortitude, faith, piety and the fear of God. It is high time that we allow ourselves to be educated in his word.

It is not a simple movement happening within us. A possible influence of mentality, it is the very power of the Holy Spirit intervening in our lives as at Pentecost. That power is dynamic enough to remove all the remnants of the past and fill us with the newness of life in the spirit. The world, your family and friends, need to know of this powerful *baptism in the Holy Spirit*. Thousands of young people, men, women, children, received the powerful touch of the Holy Spirit from their encounter with Christ. Their lives changed powerfully, they left the sterile life to assume the life of following Christ through a new behavior, now guided by prayer and its power.

That is why I invite you, with great insistence, to begin today your experience of **catharsis**, which is the emptying of yourself, the stripping of all that is unnecessary for the real development of your inner self. Repentance is full of **Kenosis**, which is an authentic breaking, physical, emotional and material, to enter into the life-giving communion that is God's own grace operating in **baptism, in the Holy Spirit**. And now I would like to tell you exactly the words that Jesus said to the Samaritan woman, **"...woman, if you knew the gift of God" (John 4)**. If we really knew the gift of God, if we were willing to enter into this mysterious garden, how many things could be different, in that garden where there is all the fullness and efficacy of God's love, reserved directly to heal us of all affliction and pain. It is the place where there is healing, where forgiveness and mercy can be found, where dignity is restored. To know God's gift is to find true protection and refuge. The garden of God is a space of faith where God himself comes to visit us to teach us new life. It is the spiritual place prepared within us to attain all the necessary knowledge and all the essential strength for you to rise as a victor. And as the father of the prodigal son said to the elder son: **"Your brother was lost and was found, he was dead and is risen, it is worthy that we celebrate him". (Luke 15:31).**

To enter this mysterious garden of God's love is to experience a real encounter with divine wisdom, with the lord of lords, with the king of kings. It is to meet again, after a life of losses, failures, abuses and so many evils, with the redeemer, the master of the vineyard, the beloved of our lives. It is to emerge from a miserable and apathetic death to be resurrected and transformed into a new creature.

For a long time I have reflected on what exactly it is to be a new creature. So many of us are accustomed to this old shell, to this old way of thinking, to outdated budgets, easily dominated by **masks and disguises** through which we hide from ourselves, from others and above all from God, the reality of our being.

Many still carry in their lives marks and deep wounds, which were left by people who cursed, harassed, slandered, smeared, discredited, assuming that because of these evil words their lives would be a real misfortune. During my priestly ministry I encountered and still encounter countless people hostage to Satan, because they allowed themselves to be trapped by these nets of curses from the past. The devil himself took hold of the words that were launched against your life so that he could dominate and deceive your path, making you believe that nothing could be done to change this history of curses. The **enemy** (evil spirit) has worked with all kinds of perversity and deception to make you believe that your life will always be useless.

That is not true. There is no greater power than that which comes from God by the manifestation of the Holy Spirit. **"In the name of Jesus, I declare the destruc-**

tion of all these curses in all your generation and the generations before you. I renounce, reject, abhor and exorcise, by the power of the blood of Christ, every satanic curse to overcome and destroy you. Be freed from your mind, your body, your emotions, so that by the grace of Jesus you may receive new life, salvation. If you believe you will see the glory of God, I summon the presence of the ministering angels of God to minister over you the anointing of protection and serve as a shield against all evil abuses. Amen."

For many years, since my childhood, I have known that God has called me as His servant, through the vocation He has placed in my life. From very early on God raised me up as a prophet of the new birth to reach out to people and announce to them the possibility of forgiveness, to begin new life, to proclaim to them the coming of God's time.

If you understand this marvelous process and you assume, accept and decide, today, *like that thief who was at the right hand of Jesus on the cross, also condemned to death and being crucified,* you can enjoy the fullness of grace and attain eternal life. *Jesus said to the thief: "Today you will be with me in paradise".* If you decide, today you can enter with Jesus in the secret of his love, in the most perfect communion. No one, absolutely nothing and no one, can separate you from this love. *"Who can separate us from the love of God that is in Christ Jesus?" (Romans 8:31).* No circumstance can take away from you this communion of sanctification and faith. Why, then, should you continue in the decision? Right now, while you are reading these lines, put your knees on the floor, raise your hands to heaven and just say to Him: *"Lord Jesus, I want to redeem myself. I want to raise my hands. Lord, I want to acknowledge, to proclaim that You are great and wonderful. I acknowledge, Jesus, how much I have failed, but now I repent and with my willing heart, I surrender myself at your feet. Come to my aid. Embrace me. Forgive me and bless me. I ask you, Lord, to make a covenant of love with me. I ask you with all my understanding to start with me a new life kept in your mercy. Impress on my hands, my heart, my mind and my soul, Lord, your most holy will. Make me your servant, kept in your divine presence".*

This is the greatest teaching gift I can give you, because in the word of Jesus I learned that *"he who seeks finds, to him who knocks it is opened, and to him who asks it is granted" (Matthew 7:8).*

There is a great desire that consumes us to experience this powerful new reality, to enter into the mystery of an expanded life, which is supposed to be a life without barriers. We are convinced that a spiritual life without barriers is exactly a barrier that has already passed through the process of the glorious encounter with Jesus.

This implies a decision in the light of the knowledge already attained, a strength capable of making a separation between the things of the past now and the things of today. The now of God is so beautiful, that it is the only force capable of enabling us, orienting us, directing us, removing from us, the co-dependence with all those things that before, for us, were indispensable. This process supposes a deep discipline of discipleship and it is very important to understand this word. It is only possible to form a person in faith when he/she makes the decision to be a disciple. A disciple is the one who is willing to begin a path of deep teaching and learning in the light of knowledge, obviously of God, but revealed to the teachers in faith; allowing oneself to enter into this communion of education, which is the power of discipleship, leads us directly, and not to a senseless obedience and deprived of our freedom as children of God.

For this reason, the relationship between disciple and spiritual master should not only be one of dependence. Both should discover, starting from the personal foundation of the disciple, his real conditions and his authentic decisions to reach the goal of conditioning to live, definitively, as an active member of the body of Christ. It is not the master who will engender the new person in God, but the master will be, and must be, an effective instrument, capable of making the whole field of the disciple well disposed to the owner of the vineyard, to the divine farmer, to God himself, who in his magnificence and mercy will graft us as true members of the vineyard that is Christ. The role of the magistrate is to lead his disciple to a deep and strict communion with Christ, where Christ will have a real possibility to connect him to his branch, that is, to lead the disciple to the fullness of the fruits.

Many people come to us in pastoral meetings, retreats, or also after mass, in moments of conviviality, and the most recurrent question and desires are: How can I produce? How can I be a more effective person in the spiritual life? The answer is always clear and categorical: Allow yourself to be a good disciple. Accept the hands of the spiritual master with obedience to the spiritual advice and discipline of life. Seek to discern at every moment the will of God in front of his projects and decisions. Unfortunately, few spiritual leaders, few clergy, few pastors, few ministers of the faith, are willing to assume this important task in the life of education in the faith, which is to form and orient people with pastoral vision, not only for the development of the mission, but also in the things that concern the restored life in Christ Jesus, leading them to experience a way of living as true persons in the light of the Gospel.

Throughout history, countless times I notice that there are courses for catechists, courses for readers of the Word of God, courses for baptismal ministers, Eucharistic ministers and a number of other courses that are offered to form leaders. Yet my question as Bishop, as shepherd of the flock of our Lord Jesus Christ is clear and pointed:

How many of these men and women are we really forming to be true and effective members of the body of Christ? How many of them are we educating in the effective experience that leads to being born again? How many of them are we teaching the need to live an effective spiritual education that produces real fruits for themselves?

Undoubtedly we must help them, through spiritual education, to seek the full consolidation of faith, until they can come to say: I am not what I do if I am not what I am, *and I am no longer who I am but Christ who lives in me*. The new normal, in accordance with the new realities of these times, awakens us to understand the new and more effective means to form people in the faith. The most effective thing we can be in our communities is that we can show the world a living and pure church, being ourselves transformed in Christ. Never a masked and hypocritical church, the essence of our being the church, the mystical body of Christ, is found not in what we do in the various services we provide, but in the originality of the faith we have and the testimony of who we truly are from the touch of Christ.

We easily throw ourselves into the arms of dreams. We hide behind the illusions of many daily events, planning, situations that, for many of us, make us believe that we are indispensable people in our communities. There are some who are so proud that they believe that without them the church will cease to exist. All this is an evident reflection that these people are centered on themselves. They are people with many talents, I recognize, but they are still absolutely nothing in the body of Christ. They are serving themselves, their own ego. *Anyone who produces outside the vine is not a member of the true vine of which we are its branches. Everything we do must be a product of what each of us is and represents in our indisputably real unity to Christ Jesus*. It is Christ who is the mystery of our work in the life of the community. Thus we express divine mercy, not by looking to ourselves, but by looking out for the welfare of our neighbor, by being good brothers to one another. This is undoubtedly the essence of our work. *It is the witness of a life enlarged by the power of God, of a life and ministry of service that encountered the mystery of God's love. To serve in the community is to diminish oneself so that Christ may appear and shine his glory in hearts. We are instruments, but it is the almighty Lord who conquers. Each servant in the work of God must assume the commitment to be to others the indelible reflection of the presence and mysterious grace of the image and likeness of God, and following the example of the community, of the apostles' deeds, be for the whole world a banner of God's love, so that when they see us they can say: "See how they love each other"*.

This love is unquestionably the force capable of moving and instilling in the heart, from the smallest to the greatest, the real sense that a community cannot live revolving around some talents of some people. The grace of God propitiates that each one of us be good dispensers of the talents that were entrusted to each of us, making them prosper according to the teaching, the discipleship and the understanding that each person receives from God's own grace. Christ himself teaches us that not all will bear the same fruit, but the most important thing is that we are not sterile and only God can fertilize in us the great work of splendid and abundant fruitfulness.

When the work of God is reaching in our space and fullness, when God begins to realize the great potential of friendship that exists between him and us, his own mercy drives us to deeper waters. He himself begins to awaken in our hearts a deep desire for more teaching, filling our soul with hope, with spiritual being, with presence with him, and he himself is giving us signs that the closer we are to this illuminating light, the more we are able to reach the knowledge necessary for our satiety and the satiety of those who are closer to us.

Many men still enjoy the unhappy experience of not building their relationship with God under firm foundations. Throughout my pastoral ministry I have met countless people with great capacities, but at the same time people weak in the capacity of understanding and submission that confuse and do not respect the teachers indicated by God. We must always keep in mind that those whom He has chosen to be spiritual teachers, it is not because they are the best or are exempt from sin, but because it is God himself who is training them and the disciple who seeks a perfect teacher, will easily be trapped by the insidiousness of Satan, which is part of the spiritual education in the disciple. The grace of obedient submission and in obedience, is the secret of the observant grace of God; He who is not capable of loving his master, he who judges as a disciple to be better than his master before having passed through the school of education, loses by his insensitivity, the grace to grow and expand on a level properly offered by the power of God.

God alone has the power to rescue and raise the human being with dignity from his miseries. He who submits himself to good discipleship and accepts to be tested in the light of God's grace through obedience to his word, will be able to surpass his master. *"Truly, truly, I say to you, he who believes in me, the works that I do he will do also, and greater works than these he will do, because I go to the Father." (John 14:12).* The first teacher is Christ. He is the head of the whole body which is the church. However, he qualifies men and women with the anointing to make disciples, with the ministry of educating God's people. Many religions, beginning with Catholicism, for a long time, until today, were very concerned with making faithful followers and few true disciples trained by the power of the Holy Spirit. It is necessary to understand the mystery of the education of the mind, to learn to discipline ourselves so that we can diminish and let Christ and His word grow in our lives. *"He must increase, and I must decrease." (John 3:30).* What a wonderful work it is to help someone live this grace, and what a great blessing to be subjected to the effectiveness of discipleship for the sake of following Christ.

Countless people are still afraid of this power. Many came to tell me: *"I am not ready to get so close to God. I don't want to keep coming to mass because of your sermons Monsignor. They are very strong and penetrate the soul. They leave me bewildered. Others told me that the God I live is very glorious and does not let them be and act according to themselves".* They are fragile souls who insist on the confused life and not on the glorious life of faith.

If you are able to remain faithful and humble to the end, in your purpose of being well educated in the grace of God, in the discipline of spiritual formation, living the sacraments of confession, holy communion, seeking daily devotional prayer and glorifying the name of God through his works, you will truly be a new person.

By the grace of God and his infinite mercy, I have had the joy of knowing the disciples who have surpassed me, and that for me is not a cause of strangeness and much less sadness, but it is a cause of inner joy. A reason to thank the Almighty, a cause of deep spiritual courage for realizing that those whom I had the courage to meet in my life and share with them the essence that was given to me by the grace of the Holy Spirit. I was able to tell them how to be formed, to have the joy today, in the midst of my weaknesses and frailties, to be able to see reflected in these same disciples the graces that are so necessary to me and now to learn with them. The essence of the disciple is in **obedience**. The essence of the master is in the **sensible and reverent humility** that never allows him to forget that the best does not come from oneself, but from someone who in all of us manifests power, authority, knowledge, mercy, compassion and grace. *The great miracle comes from Christ on the cross. It was, is and will continue to be for us the most eloquent example that death is not the end but the beginning towards redemption and eternal life.*

The true work of reconstruction of a life lies in the disciple allowing himself to legitimately adapt to the process that will widen his inner dwelling place, not in an aggressive way, but with all the light of consciousness and willing desire of his soul. To begin the work of inner reconstruction is to give yourself the opportunity to create an effective bond of intimacy with God, to allow yourself to receive the joy and eternal abundance of this glorious friendship. Inner intimacy will be able to change all your desires, which were previously animated and unwilling, into a true desire and decision to become willing and solicitous, to become studious with a strong desire to know God's own word. This desire and search for God in an educated and fruitful way, awakens a deep discipline that will lead us to bend our hearts to the light of truth. As soon as we touch the truth of God, the interior spaces of our existence will be freed from all evil and slavery, *"...and you will know the truth, and the truth will set you free". (John 8:23).*

It is time that you give yourself the opportunity to start this beautiful project of transformation. A committed action illuminated by discernment and protected by actions that are well directed and soberly oriented by the skilled hands of a good master of spiritual life, will lead you directly to spur the vices, bad behaviors, attachments, and all kinds of exacerbated things that previously dominated you. A teacher capable of working on your fragile, vulnerable and lying ego. A kind master who can go through *the valleys of shame* by your side helping you to overcome the bad past. This transformation is the work of you, of his spiritual master and definitely of the grace and power of the Holy Spirit, comforter and educator of our souls.

The power that comes from heaven, the baptism in the Holy Spirit, will fill you with vigor and will make you capable of opening yourself to the recovery of the great values that were hidden in the *ark of oblivion*.

During years of work directly linked to inner healing and deliverances through exorcisms, I met many people who were treated with very strong medicines for depression and some for others diagnosed with serious psychiatric illnesses. We really went through a painful valley with all of them, first to bring them to understand the need for healing from the inside out. More than educating them to self-knowledge, I lent them my ear and my heart to listen to them and set them free to release everything that for a long time was in their *boxes of supposed oblivion*. Many priests and many servers, most of the time, do not have enough time to attend to so many people in this way, but I am convinced that this is the path that can lead to healing. I remember when I lived in Colombia, in the mid 90's, I met many people who came from all corners of the country to experience the spiritual healing retreats we offered. They were always retreats for two hundred people and sometimes more than that. They all longed for the opportunity to have time to talk, to counsel each other and to begin a path of spiritual direction. Obviously it was impossible to attend to everyone in such a short time and dense experience to be lived. In the course of the conferences they looked at each other with spiritual hunger and thirst. They were looking for spiritual revival. They were eager to discover the power of God. Even today I remember their expressions, some with deep repentance, others with deep understanding of what they were hearing, others in awe of the power of the Holy Spirit, others weeping with gratitude to God for just being there at that moment.

In one of these meetings I met a very Catholic couple, friends of many famous priests. This couple was very prestigious and economically comfortable. They approached me and in their eyes I could see what they were looking for in that meeting. Then they told me: "We came here because some friends from Cali told us that you have a very great gift from the Lord". I did not really talk much with them, but when I looked at the lady I told her: "The baby that you want so much is already inside you. At this moment God grants you and your husband this grace and miracle". They had been trying to have a baby for years and had already undergone various treatments. They were even adoptive parents, but at that moment God opened the doors of the miracle. It is that power of the Holy Spirit that I am sharing with you now. Great things from heaven come mightily according to the intensity of faith. They had the baby. It was a great feast. They had other children and that woman, who was barren, became a fruitful woman not only to have children, but to fertilize spiritual children. And with her husband, they became even more dedicated to serve Christ through the testimony of their lives and the formation of others in the spiritual life.

The Holy Spirit blows and does so in a powerful way. We can all perceive His presence. It is the mystery of God. No one can control the movement of God's spirit. It is ineffable power. Consolation that takes and absorbs our lives, shapes and reorients our actions and emotions. The baptism in the Holy Spirit dynamically mobilizes our thinking, our way of being, leading us to assume a status and condition of newness of life. *The one who was lukewarm becomes hot. The one who was timid discovers boldness in his actions and determinations. The one who was trapped now finds himself free and determined to lead lives. The once weak, now naturally discovers an inner drive that communicates an extraordinary strength. He who was once absorbed by negativism, now finds himself seized with an authentic positive capacity. He who was rooted to impotent things, now receives a willingness to begin again.* The power of God, the anointing of the Holy Spirit, the shedding of the most precious blood of Christ upon our lives and especially in our minds and hearts, enliven our being to the dimension of the ***new being***. Therein lies the secret, to let ourselves be filled with the power of God's spirit, to find ourselves in the sacred refuge of Jesus and to develop this worthy intimacy.

Now that you are reading all this, many things are coming back to your mind and it is very good that this is so. It is a very valuable opportunity for you, in an organized way, in the light of faith and with appropriate time, to begin, ***with deep sobriety and humble and sincere intention of spirit***, to begin to organize a compilation of your own life by asking: ***Who am I? What do I bring at this moment in my consciousness? What are the things that I have hidden from the light or that I let be discarded so as not to face them?***

If you allow yourself to answer these questions with dynamic and sensitive truth, being humble with yourself, without judging and condemning yourself, it is certain that you will understand that once you are able to begin to answer them, you will feel your heart burn like never before. You will discover a thoughtful and direct movement that will bring you deep self-respect. Even if you are confronted with negative things and big mistakes from the past, situations that will bring shame, don't be discouraged, keep going. That momentary pain will propel you to discover that there is no way that evil can survive the dynamic decision to start over. When human beings give ourselves the opportunity for reflection, acceptance, forgiveness and complete healing of the conscience, is when the beginning of the true encounter with oneself and the eternal grace in Jesus Christ is given. It is that he not only finds us, but is able to bring to the one who allows himself the power of full credit. Christ returns in a grand and abundant way to one's existence. All that was stolen from us, all that was extorted from us, all that somehow made us unworthy, he now transforms to give us back the power of a healed and oriented dignity. *"I came that all may have life, life in abundance." (John 10:10). This abundance involves making manifest in us the unshakable fullness of his love. The ransom paid with his own blood on the cross. The skillful and faithful power of a grace that is constant and unchangeable. The power capable of bringing out in us the true meaning of having been created in his image and likeness.*

V. Contemplating the Restoration

"I heard of thee by the ear, but now my eyes behold thee." Job 42:5.

We are going through one of the most difficult stretches in the history of the people of God on the face of the earth in the last centuries. In the advent time of great technological discoveries, advances in science, excellent medical treatments, powerful medicines and various vaccines in full global coverage. However, the whole planet is waiting for a vaccine capable of overcoming the great challenge of a new virus, Covid-19.

A virus, under many different speculations, in which there are many controversies about its real origin. However, the same one that began to manifest itself in China at the end of 2019, already a year of its existence on the face of the earth, bringing so far more than 1.2 million dead. To you, I can imagine that this number causes enormous surprise and may shock our character. It is really very difficult to live with this reality so close to our own, we have lost very close relatives, parents, siblings, nieces, nephews, uncles, grandparents, work friends, people who had been in our lives for a long time.

We commonly hear people asking: How will we be able to beat this disease? When will we obtain a vaccine capable of protecting the entire population? Real questions, which demand efficient answers. ***In the meantime, the things of this world are subject to their own time, especially when this world has put itself first, putting aside the total surrender and consecration to God through faith***. People seek immediate answers, when they themselves, for a long time, did not care to keep their lives under the mighty hand of God. Today they cry out, but for a long time they kept their lives and that of their families, their homes, their faith, in total opposition and rebellion before God. The world suffers from the disease of not knowing, understanding that at one time it almost lost the humility of its instability and fragility in the face of adversity. It was the first time in my life that I was able to see the great scientists taken by the perplexity of not knowing how to act. We were able to see the great table of science surrender to the panic of not knowing how to treat the disease in its first cases and the chaos in the face of such a devastating situation. In hospitals and emergency rooms all over the world, they were trying and fighting like warriors to save as many people as possible. They devoted all their strength, skills and knowledge to fight against a totally unknown disease. This is the great challenge of life, to find salvation, a real answer to its first causes of existence.

What we are facing in this pandemic made us change the way of living, of relating, of connecting with the closest and the farthest people, the known and the unknown. The use of masks and other disinfecting materials made us more scrupulous. We left many friends behind, we stopped frequenting each other, we lost the bonds of immediate and physical affection, we became distant and cold. We detached ourselves from the life and commitments of the community of faith, we forgot about many people and charitable obligations, ***each one thinking of protecting and being protected.***

I would like to reflect with you now on Psalm 91.

"YOU WHO LIVE IN THE SHELTER OF THE HIGHEST
AND DWELL IN THE SHADOW OF THE ALMIGHTY,
SAY TO THE LORD: "MY REFUGE AND MY STRONGHOLD,
MY GOD, IN WHOM I TRUST.

HE WILL DELIVER YOU FROM THE FOWLER'S NET
AND FROM THE PERNICIOUS PESTILENCE;
HE WILL COVER YOU WITH HIS FEATHERS,
AND THOU SHALT FIND REFUGE UNDER HIS WINGS.

THOU SHALT NOT FEAR THE TERRORS OF THE NIGHT,
NOR THE ARROW THAT FLIETH BY DAY,
NOR THE PESTILENCE THAT LURKETH IN THE DARKNESS.
NOR THE PLAGUE THAT RAVAGES IN THE SUNSHINE.

THOUGH A THOUSAND FALL AT THY LEFT
AND TEN THOUSAND ON THY RIGHT
THOU SHALT NOT BE OVERTAKEN,
HIS ARM IS SHIELD AND ARMOR.

WITH ONLY A GLANCE
YOU WILL SEE THE PUNISHMENT OF THE WICKED,
FOR THOU HAST MADE THE LORD THY REFUGE
AND MADE THE MOST HIGH YOUR DEFENSE.

NO EVIL SHALL OVERTAKE YOU,
NO PLAGUE SHALL COME NEAR YOUR TENT,
FOR THOU HAST MADE THE LORD THY REFUGE
AND YOU HAVE MADE THE ALMIGHTY YOUR DEFENSE.

THEY SHALL BEAR THEE UP IN THEIR HANDS
SO THAT YOU WILL NOT STUMBLE OVER ANY STONE;
THOU SHALT WALK UPON LIONS AND VIPERS,
THOU SHALT TREAD UPON LIONS' WHELPS AND SERPENTS.

"HE GAVE HIMSELF TO ME,
THEREFORE I WILL GLORIFY HIM;
I WILL PROTECT HIM, BECAUSE HE KNOWS MY NAME;
HE SHALL CALL UPON ME AND I WILL ANSWER HIM.

I WILL BE WITH HIM IN DANGER,
I WILL DEFEND HIM AND GLORIFY HIM;
I WILL MAKE HIM ENJOY A LONG LIFE
AND I WILL MAKE HIM SEE MY SALVATION.

This psalm is considered the most powerful prayer in the Bible, precisely because it makes the people of God, the men and women of faith, capable of assuming the authentic posture of faith in the face of difficulties and unexpected adversities of one's existence to each one who assumes his refuge in the Lord.

In these difficult times, more than ever, this has been my daily prayer. To regain my daily refuge and restoration in the dwelling place of the Almighty. I am seeing my right and my left fall, but I am safe in the hands of the Almighty. I know that for some it is very difficult to understand this reality, but I am confident that even if you do not understand, but wholeheartedly decide to test and believe, you will not be confused in any way. The Lord will show love and mercy and bring you closer to the path of teaching necessary for your growth and development as a person in the faith and grace of God.

To keep oneself in the shadow of the Almighty is not to isolate oneself or hide oneself miserably, but to trust fully in the Lord and to keep oneself in Him, since He alone is the One who has all realities in His protection.

In recent times, especially in the most current times in which we are directly involved, the vast majority of people are hiding and seeking various shelters, but they are definitely not seeking the Real Shelter of which Psalm 91 speaks to us about. They are definitely misplaced, disoriented, frightened by the effects of the wave of despair. *When we are out of the Real Refuge and kept out of the loving mystery of God, we are totally vulnerable, it is as if we are hiding in the easy place to be caught, to be taken, to be deceived.* The purpose of this teaching is to provide you with the capable and effective tool so that each one can discover *the gentle, the good, the pleasant, the Real Refuge of being with the Lord; to enjoy the security of feeling his presence. We are his children, precious workmanship, ransomed by the blood of Christ, sanctified by the power of the Holy Spirit to fully assume the beauty of his image and likeness.*

Restoration is made from that immense love that finds us in the wasteland of perdition and protects us, guiding us to take us to His Royal Refuge, where He Himself takes care of us and heals us, so that we may be, not just recovered, but essentially restored. There, in the Real Refuge, is where the process of spiritual re-education begins, of the restitution of the losses that many of us have perhaps cast out, *in broken sacks. "Do not cast these things into broken sacks, and in the name of God command that no one be irritated in disputes which serve no purpose, but only to the ruin of those who take part in them" (2Timothy 2:14).* We are precisely talking about the bags of broken and damaged misery that let us accumulate the Lord's goods.

How many things God has taught you throughout your life, how many experiences you have had, how many moments of great enlightenment and how many were the moments of great revelation, that undoubtedly you could say: What would have happened if God had not been there with me? How would things have been if God had not nurtured me the way He nurtured me?

While some insist on continuing to throw their life and blessings into *broken sacks*, God is still, from the Royal Refuge, waiting for us to manifest to our lives the greatness of His mercy and start all over again to restore us. His immense love wants to reveal to us the potency of the gifts of the Holy Spirit, which can powerfully manifest in us the real will to live the real intensity of the spiritual life.

It is not possible for you to delay so long and continue to delay and wrongly protect yourself from the great possibility of a real leap into divine things, instead of clinging to the primarily human things that are mostly frustrating, unnecessary and disappointing. Let us put aside, as we go through life, this exhaustive effort and offer to our lives the possibility of the grace of blessing. Let us keep ourselves in the depths of the Real Refuge of God, where true restoration will be propitious to us.

I would like to take up with you one of the most beautiful texts of the Word of God, which is precisely the *encounter of Jesus with the Samaritan woman*, and I invite you to penetrate simply into the need and the depth of the dryness in which the soul of that woman found herself. The Samaritan woman is perhaps the most appropriate profile for us to draw a parallel between the frustrating experience of her life and the many frustrating, depressing and deeply suffering realities that we experience on a daily basis.

The woman here appears revealing her need for water, she was looking for it at Jacob's well. She was looking for the well that had quenched the thirst of hundreds of thousands of people for years and years. She was looking for it like all the women of her village, but not at the same time as all the women of her village. We can intuit many things, perhaps because of laziness or laziness to get up so early, or because she preferred the sun and then we realize directly her reality. She was an isolated woman, set aside from the social life of the other women in her village because of her condition of life. *She went out every day in the middle of the day, when the sun was at its hottest, precisely because she was ashamed of herself, ashamed of her life, ashamed of her condition.* I am convinced that what this woman least of all imagined that she could meet a Jew, that she could meet someone as different and deeply daring in love as Jesus. Normally at 12 o'clock in the afternoon, the well was alone, the heat was so great that no one wanted to submit to this wear and tear. So it is in life, Jesus comes to wait for us when everyone has already left, He comes at the true hour of solitude, so that we understand how much He loves us and wants to reveal His mercy to us. Such was his encounter with the Samaritan woman.

Such was the surprise of that woman when she approached the well and saw that Jesus was there. It was a total silence, one of those that communicate to us the secret of our souls. Jesus was looking into her eyes and she, surprisingly, was doing the same, clutching her still empty water pitcher. Jesus was waiting for her for a real encounter, not just to say hello, or perhaps to ignore her right away. *It should definitely be an encounter of healing, blessing and restoration.* Jesus, seeing the woman, asks her for water. I want you to understand as you read these pages of the Bible, that the Lord, in approaching us, before anything else, wants to feel our responsiveness to his presence. *In all the times that the Lord has approached me, He has asked me for something, precisely because He is the Divine Pilgrim, He Himself approaches us to know what is our disposition to share, to offer. His only need is to approach the most vulnerable and empty part of our existence to fill us with His love.*

Obviously she felt, because of her condition, an immense indignation. First of all because she was surprised by the presence of a man, a Jew, a stranger for the Samaritans, when she was quite sure of the solitude and abandonment of the place at that time of the day.

Immediately she asked the question: ***"What have I to do with you, why do you ask me for water?"*** The same is true for us in our present times, on our way of encountering Jesus, towards the restored life. When Jesus approaches each one of us, the first impulse that is born almost spontaneously and naturally, is the impulse to reject him and always because of the same thing: indignation, fear, shame, cowardice and inner darkness, the conflict that one brings against the illuminating power of the light.

"I must not give you anything, it is you who must give it to me!". As if we were saying to Jesus: ***it is you who owes me***, when in truth it is not so. ***How can you not have something to give him? How can you not approach him with your generous and sweetly disposed soul, not to question him but to offer him?*** The power of the gaze that Jesus cast upon the Samaritan woman was truly powerful to move her from all her fears and make her understand the restorative power that would be revealed through that unexpected encounter. Jesus, full of grace, said to her:

"Woman, if you knew the gift of God..." insisting, he continued, "If you knew the mystery of God, if you knew why we have met here in this place, at this warm hour of the day, in front of this Jacob's well. If you knew why we are here in this place that is so meaningful to you, to me, as it is to so many others in all eternity. By the way, if you really knew, it would not be me who would ask you for something: water, but it would be you who would ask me... as if saying to me: ***Lord, I want to enter with you in an extremely important realm, which is the realm of recognizing the gift of God, I want to be free... give me water, of your healing water, I want to lose the fear and the shame of living, I want to start a new story"***.

How many people get lost in the trickery of men, in the enchantment of the churches, of the shows, of the assemblies, of so many things that deprive the eyes, sometimes the heart, but that never change the minds and that slows down the process of life. I am trying to take you to the knowledge of the exclusive, ineffable gift of God.

If you knew the gift of God..., if you knew the greatness, the goodness, the inexorable power of the gift of God, truly everything can be changed and restored.

People tell me: ***"You have something different, they feel something different with you, your way of speaking, your way of teaching"***. Understand, this is not knowing human gifts, it is knowing the gift of God, which does not make me better, but puts me in a favored condition before the fountain of God's graces. If we were to ask Jesus: Lord, what do you want from me? Lord, what do you want me to do? Lord, where do you want me to go? Lord, how can I best present myself before you?

How can I assume this encounter with you? What exactly can I do to be faithful to the call to be at the disposal of the knowledge of God's gift? And Jesus said to that woman: "...this water that you are seeking here will satisfy you for hours and when it is finished you will have to return to this place, because this water will not quench the thirst that you bring within you. This water can only quench the thirst of your natural human need. *But, the water that I offer you is fresh water for eternal life, I will make it flow and gush within you like a spring that does not grow stagnant. I will restore your dignity, I will make you understand and know the gift of my presence, I will teach you to worship in spirit and in truth, I will not lead you to the satiety of natural needs, but I will lead you to the supernatural springs of grace, and thus, you can be fully restored".*

How many people I know who are totally blind in relation to themselves, people who have studied academic careers, technicians and even those who have gone to universities. People who have lived 20, 30, 40, 50 years, but still cannot look and search within themselves; precisely because they have not been able to know the gift of God.

When we enter into this mystery, when we understand this grace, the gift of God penetrates us in such an ineffable way, that we can not only see what is around us, but we also receive the grace to understand in order to heal all that is inside. To know the gift of God is to reach the possibility of re-evaluating all the converging facts of our history. It is to assume the commitment to realize that God is love, that his love is demanding and radical. That his powerful love can transform us. When Jesus touches us through an encounter like the one he had with the Samaritan woman, he reaches the most intimate point of our soul. He touches the neuralgic point, which is very important, extraordinary and potentially the source of our being, it is where the true code of who we really are lies. It is the point of weakness that is not misery, that is not vulnerability, but is the real essence of our image and likeness in which we were created and by sin denigrated, losing our real connection with the origin of the love in which we were created. When Jesus asks that woman: *"Whom are you going to look for?* If you really have no one to look for, if in your reality you have five husbands, which husband do you refer to?"

At that moment the woman realized that Jesus knew not only her heart, but deeply and diametrically, he knew everything that populated around her social, material and conjugal history. *To enter into the knowledge of God is to discover the way by which it becomes possible for us to enter into the intimacy of his mystery that opens itself to us in a singular and individual way. It is to let God know what is populating around us, each component of our roots, the way in which our choices, decisions and life itself were built and developed. It is to open our hearts in such a way that God is revealed in the reality of each one of us, it is to open to Him the possibility of experiencing the thirst of our daily water.*

The woman leaves her pitcher and goes out to meet the people of her village. She leaves the pitcher, she leaves the water of Jacob's well, the thirst of the body, the domestic chores, she leaves her way of life. She leaves the old necessities and frees herself from the shame that made her hide. Now she runs out, not without meaning, but now with a mission: the testimony of her own life. She goes forward without fearing whom she will meet along the way.

After the restoring encounter with Christ everything changes, everything becomes new. Arriving in the city, her impulse of faith and new life made her cry out without fear of being judged, because all condemnation had been left in the jar abandoned by Jacob's well. With a strong voice and spirit spirit she said: *"Come, come, come all of you who are silent, who are deceived, come all of you who are unbelieving, because I have met the master, a man who has not only brought me peace, but who knows everything about my life, knows everything about my past, knows my history and has given me more than all have offered me. He has given me the grace to know the potency of his love and his power."*

It is this intimacy that I am sharing with you with so much love and faith, an intimacy that is not generated by superficial interests, but is born of an intimacy, the fruit of true connection with the love of Christ. To connect to God, is to connect with Jesus in the hidden mystery, is to find the Real Refuge, to be part of the secret of love. It is to discover that we bring in our very fragile humanity, the unceasing desire to encounter the healing and redeeming power of our Lord Jesus Christ.

Close your eyes so that at this moment you may ask Jesus for this grace to happen in your life, tell him: *"Lord, great has been the time of shame, of degradation, of humiliations, of judgments, in which I have hidden myself, in which I have put myself behind traps, of lies, deceiving myself, harming myself and my fellow men, trying to lead a double life looking for water only from the water of momentary pleasures. Lord, wait a little, I am realizing, that there is a spring of living waters, I know Lord, that the Holy Spirit blows where He wills and how He wills. Lord, I know also, that you seek worshipers, who worship you in spirit, in truth, therefore I want to offer myself Lord, before the grace to know you, through a real intensity, with unwavering truth, with a heart willing to be transformed and restored. Take possession, Lord, of all these things and pour upon me the blessed and loving efficacy of your heart. Only you can help me, only you can give me a new name, only you can lead me back to a new reality before and around those who knew me in the past. I know Lord, that you deny no one an opportunity and I want to be a witness of this opportunity of love, I want to be worthy of this opportunity of blessing, I want to be one of the transformed flags in your hands. I, who before was a pirate flag, a flag of error, a flag branded by evil, now I want to be a clean flag, a white flag with the sign of your love, of your cross. I want to be a person transformed in your most precious blood. Blessed and praised be you Lord, glorified be you Lord, adored may you be".*

If you have been able to understand what I have said and expressed through this last prayer and have been able to pray deeply with me, you are certainly now enjoying a special encounter of restoration. It is impossible to go through this process without touching and being touched by the power of God, without knowing the immeasurable gift of knowing God in his mystery of love.

I want to direct you to a new vertex of this very special encounter with Christ, after the intimacy, it is necessary to develop good communication which will make us understand not only our personal experience, but also learn to realize, to discover how to listen, how to scrutinize, how to feel the probes of God's manifestation in our existence.

Samuel was still a child in the house of the High Priest and God called him: *"Samuel, Samuel",* and the child, in spite of hearing the voice, was not yet able to distinguish whose voice it was and where it really came from. The child was still not able to distinguish who, why and for what purpose he was called. This phenomenon happened as many as three times, until Samuel was able to say: *"Here I am, Lord".*

How many times has God called you, how many times has God placed very clear signs before you, how many times has God revealed himself to your ears, to your eyes, to your senses and you still remained in total ignorance? It is the difficulty of communication that you must also learn to develop.

The growth of Christ in us makes us capable of assimilating into our existence, realities that transcend our own communication potentials. Communication is more than information, true communication must lead us totally to the dialogue of communion, be it with ourselves, our fellow men and even more, with God. I have many friends who recurrently come to me and very intimately tell me their stories. Some tell me in the course of the topic: *"I never thought I was capable of doing what I did at that particular moment in my life, but I felt that there was a force within me that drove me, a capacity that transcended my abilities, a love that led me fascinatingly to love as I had never loved before".* This is the disposition of this intimacy with full communication between the one who is the interlocutor and the one who is the author, the almighty Lord, who through you wants to proclaim great works and splendid wonders. This is the great triumph of the powerful life of communion and communication with God.

St. Francis of Assisi, in the canticle of praise says: *"Make me, Lord, an instrument of your peace, where there is hatred, may I bring love, where there is doubt, may I bring faith, where there is despair, may I bring hope, where there is war, may I bring peace; O Master, make me capable of consoling more than being consoled, of loving more than being loved, for it is by giving that one receives and it is by forgiving that one is forgiven".*

I believe that no one, like St. Francis of Assisi, knew how to understand the great mystery of this full communication of God's closeness to us, in order to make each one of us bridges for the proclamation of grace: to love more than to be loved, to understand more than to be understood, to forgive more than to be forgiven. To go out of the foreground to leave to God the place that belongs to Him. *If someone says he loves you, but does not love God, he is a liar and every form of love that does not have the seal of God's love can never be recognized as true love.* God is love and every expression of love comes from Him, in Him and with Him.

Be strong enough to understand today that if there is in you any kind of love that does not have its origin in the redeeming and restoring love of God, that love is a fraud, a lie, an invention of Satan to impassion your soul and to blind your sense of faith. Love is born of God, it is God Himself, God is God! Love is God, God is Love! He who loves God, he who believes in love, that same love manifests itself in him as a force of liberation and blessing. God is love, the source of love, the principle of love, eternal love. We are born of him, in him we exist and when we die in this same love, we will live eternally kept in the love of loves, Christ Jesus to the eternal resurrection.

VI. Into the deep sea toward the New

"And when he had finished speaking, he said unto Simon, Set sail into the deep, and let down your nets for a catch. Simon answered and said to him: Master, we have labored all night and caught nothing; but on thy word I will let down the net". Luke 5:4-5.

It is very important and interesting, in a way, to compare the different theories on the subject throughout human history. This from the most ancient times, at the end of the 19th century, to the middle of the 20th century, and finally to observe the latest discoveries about matter, mechanics, quantum physics and philosophy itself. It is interesting to analyze all that to be convinced that scientific ideas, from time to time, change and present new ones to each generation.

Similar revolutions can be observed in all fields and objectives of the various sciences, we could underline physics, astronomy, theology, medicine and especially in the newest sciences, such as psychology, which is still trying to find its full and wide space in the field of sciences.

What yesterday was considered unquestionable truth (dogmas), today is already rejected and put to the test of doubt under the magnifying glass of new judgments and understandings always scientifically oiled.

When new scientists become popular for their new discoveries, the old ones are easily lost in oblivion as advances in the field of science in general are made, as if they were almost outdated. Perhaps this is the greatest trap of science, the constant need for advancement and updating, almost insurmountable, which makes the one who is its lover, a follower not for the maintenance of the same, but in a tireless discoverer of new points, elements that do not let him fall into oblivion or nullity. We can easily compare this scientist to a man who runs by leaps and bounds over ice plates in an immense glacial sea, each ice plate is a point of access, but never of permanence, the one who walks cannot stop, because scientific progress demands a dynamic movement that overcomes inertia at every instant. To jump and continue discovering is absolutely necessary, to remain stagnant is impossible. No discovery, no matter how excellent it may be, is insurmountable and science itself only persists as long as it continues to be a gateway to new discoveries. The power of faith does not force us in any way, or to work in the field of the creation of ideas of principles or behaviors, the only sense of faith is to make each believer reach the level of harmony between the natural and the supernatural, taking into account the power of the grace of following Jesus Christ, of the reading of prayer, of the word of God as essential peace for the engendering of our being, of a new potential of autonomous capacity, of perspectives. If you cannot be of perspective, it is because you are still jumping from reality to reality, believing that faith is only a means of discovery.

I am sure that faith does not make us discover, because faith itself leads us to the mystery of the contemplation of things that do not yet exist on our material plane and that are not yet under our physical eyes, since they are in themselves full and capable in the supernatural plan of God's grace.

So what to do when science has no answer and we also realize that what we expect in faith does not answer us either?. That is a great dilemma in the life of spiritual faith, the fact that we believe to have great faith in God will never make our perspectives to be exactly the same of God. Each one of us has come to this history, to this time in which we live, with a mission and the effective man by the power of faith filled with the love of God, Each of us has to learn throughout our lives, through the power of faith, that God is a God of providence, that He sees before any of us are able to see and His providence manifests in our souls the necessary capacity to assume daily in us His divine will. This is a life of unity and communion.

Do not be deceived, science will never have a definitive word to faith, everything can be changed by the power of God's grace, where I can no longer, the spirit of God continues to act. God always works in silence, without disturbing or distracting us, his love of immense providence is capable of doing without human mediation, by his own infinite grace, immeasurably more than what we think, what we desire and what we expect. *For this reason, put on your faith the decisive power of things, make of it an instrument that maintains its capacity to love and adore God above all things and situations. In the midst of difficulties learn to give thanks, learn to glorify. In the face of unexpected misfortunes and tragedies, proclaim in your soul the unquestionable greatness of the Lord. Raising your hands and your voice full of faith, invoke with authority the powerful name of Jesus, who is the source, beginning and end of all your existence.*

Throughout my life, the Lord has easily given me the opportunity to be tested in the ability to live from faith, from the expectant experience of his holy and divine will. I remember in the beginning of my spiritual walk of faith, I easily cried and prayed to God as an insistent, inconsequential child. Today, after much incessant asking, God has given me the grace to understand the effective way to turn to at the time of intercessory prayer. His own love directed me how to ask and when it is really time to ask through the power of intercession. I learned through the falls to understand clearly what, even if I ask, will not be granted to me, because God does not probe my will to fulfill my desires, but God probes my need to honor in my humanity the mystery of His holy will. God alone is holy, God alone is most high, and God does not please us for the aggrandizement of ourselves, but God makes manifest in us, by the power of our faith, the eternal work of his merciful faithfulness. God is not faithful to my faith nor to your faith, God is faithful to the covenant of love, to the covenant of goodness that He has established on the cross in Christ Jesus. Everything is born of the atoning power of Jesus on the cross.

It is not only asking, one has to belong to Jesus, one has to shape one's existence in the existence of Jesus, and with that faith make the right use of the powerful name of Jesus. We must not, in any way, usurp the mystery of the glorious name of our Lord Jesus Christ, He died for us when we were still sinners and the grace of God in us is so great, that if we in Christ die, in Him we will rise again. To pray with faith in the name of Jesus and to ask the Father through the intercessory power of Christ, is proof of true faith and spiritual life. Anyone who keeps, protects and shelters himself in the cross of our Lord Jesus Christ, preserves his mystery and the power of his name in his own life, becomes a person powerfully protected by the grace of heaven. This has been my experience throughout my life after so many falls and so many defeated fragilities. Little by little the Lord has taught me that I cannot lose sight, not even for a day, of the expectation of dying in Him so that in Him I can attain to live in fullness of grace. To be a bearer of faith is to live the mystery of the passion, death and resurrection of our Lord Jesus Christ every day and in every circumstance of our existence, in each of our trials, in each of our problems. In every prayer, in every sacrament, in every moment of strong intercession. In the face of various situations, do not focus only on the misery of the circumstances, but try to center your actions on the power of faith.

No one can deny that the comparison between faith and other human abilities is a reality, we could say about intuition, the potential capacity of human reasoning. *Faith gives each of us real access to that which is humanly intangible through the bodily, physical and emotional senses*. In this way, thanks to faith, we are able to arrive at the conviction that the reality in which we are engrafted is minimally contemplated in relation to the reality of the things held in faith by its eternal power.

All these things exist through the sapient power of the creator, God is infinite wisdom, he created us and potentially gave us an immortal soul so that we could share with him the eternal and blessed life. In fact, faith is often present in all areas of scientific discovery, even if the scientismists do not have it in this enlightenment perspective. If we look at the Big Bang theory, which is, for scientists, the origin of the creation of the universe, we perceive exactly that the force of the Big Bang is energy and not matter and we also perceive that from this theory, other worlds different from ours could exist and all this leads us to a very strict concept that has nothing to do with the breadth that faith gives us.

Thanks to the contact with God, we who believe, receive a special recognition of the truth, which is an inner faculty to perceive the greatness of God's love and that reason is still unable to understand only in the light of science. For example, we could say the resurrection of the dead, the final judgment, eternal life. All these things, in addition to the experiences of everyday life and other verifications of the reason of life, we perceive the realities that definitely by faith are to be fulfilled. *Definitely, the power of faith gives us the special perspective of a different look and helps us surely to see beyond the apparent logical horizon.* But it is important for you to understand that even an ultra-sensitive eye cannot see without the aid of light. The best microscope needs light. Any eye needs light. Similarly faith needs the divine light of revelation. It is the very light of grace that guides our faith into fruitfulness and abundance of resources of blessings.

This is the most magnificent thing we can understand through this book. Our life in God, our love for God and our faith guided by God's love needs light. Every man and woman who truly desires to live by faith and kept in faith must have par excellence in their hearts the power of light. It must be discovered what quality of light each one brings in himself. It is Christ, *not an energy, not a kind of light*, but *Christ is the energy, Christ is the light, nothing will exist and nothing can be apart from Jesus Christ. Hallelujah*, He is the light of the world!

We want to talk about the ability to believe and think that faith is beyond physical knowledge, really because we have understood that faith will never exclude logical thinking. Many people, for centuries, have tried to make a dichotomy of what is meant by a cut-off, a separation, between faith and the capacity of reasoning, as if trying to relate believing people to unenlightened people, referring to faith as alienating them. For a certain time faith was understood as an alienation to knowledge and true enlightenment.

What an incredible thing to think and imagine, but to have faith, more than anything else, is to enter into the depths of knowledge and to seek the intimacy of enlightenment in order to embrace things that are not seen and to hope for things that are still outside the reality of the present time. It is therefore impossible to speak of matters of faith to the exclusion of natural realities and the possible faculties of human knowledge, it is not our purpose to presume that faith is more important than knowledge, but we are definitely willing to understand that both faith and knowledge arise from the same principle that makes all things manifest the fullness of God's glory.

How we enjoy looking at a work of art, how we enjoy attending a talk with someone fully enlightened, lucid, full of knowledge, techniques and methodological possibilities to make us understand. How it fills our spirit when we observe the different works of engineering, as it is when we cross a beautiful bridge over a river, how many beautiful skyscraper buildings make us admire how far the capacity of man can reach when he allows himself to think, imagine and challenge himself. It would be total brutality and ignorance to think that such great things and discoveries were somehow able to reach all these excellent levels if they were not illuminated in the minds of people who truly gave space for their minds to be illuminated and transported to the level of originality and creativity, if they were not guided and sheltered by the light of the challenge greater than the very connection existing in themselves and in science itself.

Science will always be ready to be developed, as long as there are men willing to give it value and find its timely capacity of expression from new discoveries, but there will never be science and there will never be faith, if every man and every woman are not previously awakened to this unfathomable world of unfathomable possibilities. No one can believe and no one can think if they have not been awakened by the transcendent light that makes them see the potential beyond the superficial and be able to desire to make of this potential a powerful capacity to inspire themselves and others who discover it, thus beginning an endless cycle of discovery processes that lead them to others, as well as to many other diverse possibilities. Science is also full of spectacular and mutually generated encounters.

So then, faith and knowledge must walk, not in a disconnected way, but faith and science must walk hand in hand, one serving the other and both serving the good of God's creation. *For not only faith, but also knowledge, both can reach limitless spaces, provided that before them precedes them the fire of the light that does not go out, the glorious flame capable of leading, not to themselves, but to the restorative and creative good that leads all action to others, to those most in need of their direct and indirect actions.*

Faith that is individualistic, such as knowledge that is closed in on itself, is worthless and of no service, emptying itself in itself without any kind of efficacy. Knowledge and faith in an exuberant and real way, must be given the continuous opportunity of service to the good of others and their productive maintenance so that its manifestation reaches the service of others and there is growth in the most diverse levels of existence.

To have faith is not to boast, to have knowledge is not to usurp in pride and self-satisfaction. To enjoy the benefit of faith and knowledge, both simultaneously, is an acquired grace, a power that comes down directly from the privilege of God's blessing, from the favor of God's own love, as King Solomon experienced, to receive the knowledge and light that came from the high heavens. This is to experience the power that is directly intended for men and women who are willing to the light. Where faith is manifested there is no gloom, where there is knowledge and this knowledge is enlightened by the power of wisdom, there can never be disturbance or disturbance. Knowledge propels us to renewing levels of existence and enables us to advance and progress with abundance of actions.

All that there is and even causes contradiction as far as their judgment is concerned, must be illuminated, not only by the light of morality, because morally we are all corrupted and we cannot be partial. The judgment of things and their qualification must enjoy profound ethics, of a strict character, meticulously guarded by the force of truth. Jesus Christ is the truth, He alone knows the truth in its fullness, that is why He is seated at the right hand of the Father. The judgment of science and of faith itself will never be found in chains, Jesus said: *"You will know the truth and the truth will set you free" (John 8:32)*. Every time I hear this word or read it, meditate on it in my heart, my whole soul is filled with faith and knowledge. It is impossible for a person to read and hear these words without a natural desire to experience the truth of God and in God.

Christ is the truth, and he who has faith must come to Him. Those who do not yet have faith must struggle to exercise the victory of the virtues against the vices on the path of purification, in order to free themselves from so many unnecessary things. Freed from all chains and bonds you can enter the field of faith and knowledge. He who despises knowledge will never understand the need to perceive the difference between light and darkness, intelligence and ignorance, *knowledge is the powerful force that can activate in man the impact of truth, the blow of abundant light. When someone knows something or someone very shocking, he is awakened by the force of his inner light, because what he discovers is truly good and capable of the potential to change realities, he discovers what is good and admires its potential. No one hides a light under the bed. No one can hide something wonderful in the eyes of the righteous and sensible of heart.*

Be assured that all things that are hidden will be revealed and it is Christ who will reveal them by the force of his power. If you have the need to understand, to know, to discern and to approach science, do not be afraid; all these things are possible to men and women who believe, to men and women who have faith, to those who are willing to rise above and overcome all obstacles through faith and knowledge.

It is definitely a wonderful thing, knowledge gives us infinite opportunities, but without faith nothing is possible. It is necessary to believe in yourself, it is necessary to believe in life, it is necessary to believe in the things that are around you. It is very important to believe with all the strength of existence and all the power of knowledge so that our testimony may be a reflection of God's grace, which is fully manifested in us and potentially desires to be manifested in the hearts of those we love the most.

Real and authentic knowledge, if it is not filled with humility, loses its essential meaning, loses its capacity to penetrate, loses its efficacy of development. I like to give the example of the peacock, all his beauty is not only seen in the beautiful cadence of his walk or when he flies towards the treetops or even when he gives his morning call, his beauty is fully seen when he walks in the fields and discovers someone, he wants to show himself and decides to make visible all the beauty that was hidden before, he reveals himself. How many of us have not been moved by the beauty of the exposed plumage of the peacock, seeing the splendor of his feathers? What beauty, what richness of detail, what colors, how could creation capture something so particular, so excellent, with such nobility and at the same time with such simplicity?

Faith makes us transcend in us the deep desire to contemplate things that are beyond our human advantages, beyond our physical, mental and emotional capacities. Faith makes us understand the real existence of God and that He is omnipotent and existent and that His operation transcends the capacity of our hands and material operations. Faith enables us to understand that there is a ***powerful breath*** capable of making inert things reach a vibration as powerful as if they were alive. It is similar to what happens to us when we look at a photograph, especially of a person we love very much and who is far away, perhaps in another country or sometimes in another city or perhaps already dead; it is faith that allows you to feel that that photograph speaks to you, it is as if you could communicate and receive affection from that inert photo and in an intimate way be able to experience living feelings, enter into such a special moment capable of sharing things that had never been possible in person. It is faith that allows us to dialogue with silence, the power of the breath of the Holy Spirit that moves and transforms.

How many times people come to me with photos in their hands for me to pray for people I have never seen and never met. Photos at healing masses of people with whom I never had any kind of contact. Photos of people with different stories and situations, but when we look at the photo, the Lord gives us through the breath of the Holy Spirit the gift of knowledge of science, which allows us to look at the photo and see what the Lord himself wants to reveal to us for prayer and intercession and definitely miracles happen. In many circumstances, the person didn't even take the picture and through the gift of science, God enables us to see what is happening and describe the person and proclaim their deliverance and healing. It is definitely faith united with the grace of knowledge placed at the service of the brethren. Thus God makes manifest the mystery of grace, that which is hidden in the blessing of priestly hands and in the hands of so many other instruments of faith.

I would like you to understand the powerful force of faith, which, in the face of the black veil of ignorance, can powerfully overcome the smoke of fear and reveal the miracle. The healed mentality and the faith supported by prayer and the word of God, makes us unconditionally different, endows us with a grace that separates us from the great mass of barely natural people, exalts us to the grace of living the supernatural of God's goods and promises. *If you really want to be a different person, do not concern yourself with the things of your stereotype, with the way you dress, speak, pray, sing, lay on your hands, just concern yourself with keeping yourself in the presence of the Lord, with being humble, a good vessel for every good work, a willing instrument for the grace of God to penetrate your inmost heart and thus allow this wonderful power to fertilize in you a new personality, now illuminated by the knowledge of the spiritual beatitudes.*

This very morning, while I was praying, I had the grace, in the midst of the praises and intercessory prayer that I do every day, to receive from the Lord a word of spiritual knowledge through faith, I could feel, perceive, understand and penetrate strongly in the presence of God. With miraculous faith I was able to advance in the depth of the dialogue with the Lord, it was a time of fruitful abundance and intimacy. Faith moves us, as it is capable of moving a mountain from one side to the other, as Jesus told us: *If only your faith were like a mustard seed*, tiny but powerful, knowing its capacity, a very tiny mustard seed, minuscule, but powerful and aware of its power. In spite of its smallness, it brings in its inner identity the excellent greatness of its mission: to grow and grow. Many things would be different in your life if you really understood your original mission, your identity, the meaning for which you were created and called to life. How can you believe that someone believes in you if you yourself do not know who you are? How can you be respected if you yourself do not believe in you? How can you want people outside your home to respect their children, their family, if you yourself do not believe in them, if you yourself look at them with discredit, with incomprehension? It will be impossible.

Hundreds of people have approached me throughout my life and have told me with tears the deep feeling with which they came to disgrace and were totally lost in their lives because they were discredited. People who have within their minds and feelings, words of denial because they heard them from their parents, their relatives, their partner, their closest friends. They were imprinted on them in the form of wounds, that they could never achieve their goals, that they would never be respected, that they would never have opportunities. These people were robbed of their ability to believe in themselves, something was taken away from them and they were left blind waiting for an awakening by the grace of God. *For years they lived wildly, inconsistently, and incoherently. They are those people we know, who live with us or are part of our social life, people who tried for years and in different ways to solve their challenges in their own way, without ever opening up to others, precisely because they were deeply wounded and lost the ability to believe in themselves, in others and above all in God. These people can only be healed if they approach the fire of God, the light of the Almighty.*

Many of these people came to me in one way or another and by God's grace I was able to help them experience with me to trust in God. It is not easy, but no one told us it is impossible. We have to try and be faithful in the service of healing out of love, with faith and knowledge in God's grace. As the disciples learned to trust Jesus in the midst of the storm, they attentively watched when Jesus commanded the winds and the waves of the sea to calm down, just as the disciples realized that Jesus had splendorous dominion over nature, these people close to my life and ministry, realized that they needed faith and knowledge to be healed. On one occasion my secretary said to me: "Monsignor, so many people that I know do not have faith, how can these people live, how can they subsist?" My answer to her was direct and incisive: "He who does not have faith will succumb sooner or later, because ignorance of God, ignorance of his grace, ignorance of his power, prevents us from crossing over to true life. God is on the other side of the river and there are many people who still insist on believing that there is only life on this side of the river. When problems arise, when storms come, these people who are on this side of the river begin to succumb and those who have taken the time to know the truth in Christ Jesus through faith and knowledge, build through the very cross of Christ a saving bridge to the other side of the river, where there is peace, where there is serenity, where there is real refuge, where there is endless encounter. The power of faith and trust in knowledge that comes down from the high heavens, allows us to cross the river and walk through the cross of Christ, to be healed, liberated, restored, for having been able to renounce himself, all the benefits of a superficial life full of sins, to take upon himself his own cross and declare by faith the fight against the vices and evil of corruption, recognizing the goal of living on the other side of the river, where there is communion with God".

I want to bless you this moment and ask God our Lord to put these two truths in your heart, faith and knowledge. *Faith cannot be ignorant and knowledge cannot be mediocre.* We need our faith to be lucid and our knowledge to always remain nailed to the truth that is Christ.

I ask God our Lord at this moment to touch your heart and your mind to enlighten your inner being with the light of the gospel, to enlighten your whole being with the powerful light of grace, to enlighten your spirit with the power of truth and may the Almighty bring to you the beginning of peace, that you may find peace in the heart of Jesus, that you may discover that Jesus is with you in the boat, on the mighty way that will bring you redemption to the fullness of communion. May Jesus, who is your magnificent Lord, come to manifest deep love upon you, may the Lord touch your mind with enabling light and lead you to maturity of spirit. May the Lord touch your inner self and make you understand the truth of your existence. In the name of the +Father, the +Son, and the +Holy Spirit. Amen.

I will share with you an experience:

It was 11 o'clock at night, when a father of a family, here in our church, called me on the phone, he immediately sent me a text saying: "My daughter left the house", immediately I was woken up, frightened, I began to pray. I could not contain the pain in my heart, I felt a pain in my head and for an instant I was able to feel the pain in the heart of that father. I have known that family for 10 years, I know the girl's father, whom I myself helped to leave the dependency he had in the past and now I was helping him to save his family, his children.

Before hanging up the phone I said to the father: "God is going to bring the girl back home". It is this faith that we are talking about and this knowledge that surpasses human material capacity. The first thing I found on the phone in the morning was a message saying: "my daughter is already with us" and with deep gratitude to the Lord, I shouted loudly: Glory to God, and went to church in order to work".

Genuine faith is that which has the glorious power of light. It is Christ who reveals it to our hearts, it is Christ who makes known to us each stage in our process of maturing in faith. Believing is not just finding a stable place for devotional life or a quiet environment of prayerful refuge, or a kind of place of isolation in itself.

Genuine faith does not deprive us of the impulses of everyday life. It always directs us toward an encounter with the light. Believing in a mature and simple way arouses in the believer a continuous and renewable dynamic force towards the deepest waters of the divine ocean. He who truly believes, with authenticity and real meaning, never surrenders the leadership of his existence to laziness or to the weak and susceptible naivety of the mind. There are many people who believe that faith is to stop accompanying the course of life and live trapped in the tradition of other experiences that others had and that others lived. This is not so, one of the most beautiful characteristics of faith is that it updates us in the present mystery, in spite of all the challenges and failures of the present, it does not allow us to stop looking at the mystery of God and his immense power to intervene in our history at any moment.

My faith is a reflection of the faith of Abraham, of the faith of Isaac, of the faith of Jacob, of the faith of the patriarchs, of the kings, of the judges of the prophets. It is that which is born of the testimony of the faith of the apostles, of the authenticity of Peter and Paul, of the martyrs such as St. Stephen and the Christians who gave their lives to the scourge and to the lions in the sands. The faith of the saints like St. Benedict, St. Augustine, St. Bernard, St. Francis, St. Padre Pio, St. Rita, St. Gemma Galgani, St. Charles Duarte Costa, the faith of the silenced saints. I am a witness to the faith, a man born for the glory of God. He has called me, chosen, consecrated and sent me to be in this century, starting from the great challenges contrary to the faith, a Bishop with testimony, teaching and authority to form men and women through the effective capacity and possibility existing in the human being to believe in God. I am convinced, from my own ministry, that faith must be communicated from heart to heart through the preaching of the word of God. *"Faith comes by hearing the word of God." (Romans 10:17).*

In the face of a society that still marginalizes, discriminates, that still enslaves minds, that is still racist, misogynist, that still makes exceptions for people, genders, cultures, ethnicities, that still is not able to recognize that we are members of one another, we must be able to preach the power of faith and the potency of the word of God. The witness of God's word touches us and saves us if we truly listen and allow its power in us as it is proclaimed to assume the authority to pierce deeply into our souls. It is in this century of countless contrasts that God has raised me up as Bishop of a simple and materially poor community, it is here in Long Beach, California, in the United States of America, that God calls me to be an apostle of faith and knowledge. Here he has humbly raised me up to be an instrument of truth, here he has renewed my gifts and charisms, to be a man according to his holy and divine will. By his infinite mercy, he has called me to bring the illumination of the light of Christ in the midst of the darkness that drowns us, which is our own current systemic selfishness. God's grace has called me to lead people to inner healing, to the path of reencounter with themselves and with God's own mercy.

Our faith, my faith, your faith, must be coherent and we must recognize that to follow Christ is to assume the vocation of king, priest and prophet, that means to be called, by the grace of God, to recognize that in us is the Holy Spirit, whose temples we are. Each baptized and confirmed in the faith, assumes the mission of being salt of the earth and light of the world. It is no longer possible for us to live in an aligned way, outside and distant from the identification and testimony of genuine faith.

Our witness, which is the witness of the church itself, the body of Christ, must not just be reduced to words from the mouth to the outside, but must be filled with the spirit of new life, which implies a true way of evangelization, reflecting a way of life that is whole and real, that proclaims Christ and not ourselves. In each of the realities and systems that surround us, reasoning and faith should help us to create an authentic perception between what is truth and what is illusion.

A quiet and calm reflection about the truth and the faith we live by will help our witness to create a strong foundation and an irreproachable base. What I find most distressing to see in the people with whom I interact in the pastoral and ecclesial sphere is precisely to perceive in them the fear of the truth, the difficulty of facing their own reality through the truth, whatever it may be. This reveals the lack of foundations in the experience of faith and above all the lack of security in the benefits of charity among brothers and sisters. Many of the people who proclaim themselves to be bearers of great faith are not yet capable of enjoying an exercise of their own conscience. When good priest, confessor or spiritual director, begin visiting and scrutinizing with them their inner dwellings, which according to them are great structures that speak of their faith, we realize that for years they built without solid and original foundations, they lived a lot of time of other people's experiences and nothing concrete was done. *It is very important to discover and investigate if the faith that you bring inside you is really a product of the truth that is Christ or if it is just a great religious illusion, fruit of something that you drew in your religious imagery. This is a great challenge to be worked on and overcome, to help our brothers and sisters to be able to abandon the lifestyle based on a variant and illusionary faith, with the objective of living an authentic and well-founded experience of faith.*

The great problem of people who live their faith illusorily, is their susceptibility, instability and vulnerability in the face of adverse circumstances. Precisely, I am talking about their weakness in having to face with knowledge and true faith the great problems that confront our lives. It is at this moment that they collapse, fall, despair, lose control. Their souls are not well solidified, the faith they bring is illusory faith, barely religious, based on other people's experiences. They do not really know the Lord, they have not built a solid interior dwelling, their interior is like dust, like a sand castle, easily destroyed.

Jesus Christ never taught us to live a blind faith, on the contrary, Jesus when speaking to the apostles and disciples made mention of emphasizing the need for each of them to seek a foundation for their faith, in the scriptures themselves Jesus told them: *"Examine the scriptures, it is they that testify of me" (John 5: 39)*, he also suggests that those who were not believers, to examine the miracles so that they would be convinced of the divinity of his ministry: *"But if I do them, though ye be-*

lieve not me, yet believe the works, that ye may know and believe that the Father is in me, and I in the Father" (John 10:38). In the same way the apostles invited the early Christians to make use of reason and discretion concerning matters of faith: *"Beloved brethren, do not believe ignorantly, but test the spirits, to know whether they are of God", (1 John 4:1). "Though ye believe not me, yet believe the works, that ye may know and believe that the Father is in me, and I in the Father", (2 Timothy 1:13 - 4:3).*

With this emphasis I am moving towards the end of this matter between faith and reason, making it explicitly clear that we cannot in any way put in confrontation both realities, they complement each other and one proves the existence of the other.

Faith leads us to knowledge and knowledge invites us to faith, this unity of two such strong realities makes us understand that reason is to search, to prove and to substantiate, reason protects faith against the illusions of humanity, against the great error of distortion and fanaticism. Faith, on the other hand, is the driving force that opens new horizons in the growth of the relationship between creation and creator, to each one who is filled with it and in it is fulfilled, discovers the effective means to be taken out of the superficial life, of the smallest and properly human realities, so that it, the authentic faith in the divine mystery, can elevate us and transport us towards the supernatural and divine realities. *Faith can be compared to an engine and reason to a guide wheel, without the engine the cart does not move but without the guide wheel it can crash, it is important that you understand that no wild way of existing can take you where you want and have to go.*

You must understand as soon as possible, that freedom effectively seeks and needs faith and knowledge, when we can live these two realities in harmony, not only does a dynamic hope and a powerful love for service develop in us, but also a genuine capacity for connection with God develops in us.

It is then possible to speak with the almighty through his word and his many teachings, that is to be able to join the experience from knowledge with the experience from faith and make these two realities become a full space of abundance and love in God, with God and towards God.

VII. The Call to the True Surrender of Life

"I stand at the door and knock, if anyone hears my voice and opens the door
I will come in to his house and dine with him and he will dine with me."
Revelation 3:20.

Through these beautiful words, our Lord makes us know the interest that is born of His own love and desire to seek us in any way. He himself comes, he wants to question us. He is aware of our idleness and our difficulty in understanding his divine will. He offers himself to each one of us out of his infinite providence and compassion. He is the Good Shepherd who seeks his sheep and wants to meet each one of us in our particular circumstances. He comes to each door, without making differences of any nature, his objective is to meet each one who wishes to open the door.

It is we, individually and personally, who are invited to open the door. His coming does not force us or wish to cause us any kind of misfortune. He knocks on our doors, our connections, our points of convergence, our relationships, He wants to be part of our intimacy, to reach into our inner world, He wants to start a serious relationship of love.

We have something very considerable which is the free will, the power, the autonomous faculty of each one to accept or reject, to desire with nature of conscience or with whim of stubbornness whatever it is that tinges our existence. This subject encloses the most tenuous and fragile point of our choices and great decisions, positive or negative.

Many people still retain the idea that God is a God who persecutes, who mistreats, a God who allows suffering and catastrophes. This vision is totally wrong, God is love. Love does not punish, does not cause mistreatment and never destroys. However, the subjects, who are us in the struggle to reach love, cause a series of disasters because of our ignorance and we end up blaming love itself for our inabilities and inconsistencies. In spite of all that, love does not change, it continues to love and to desire to be loved.

God is kind and genuinely willing to reach out to each one of us, he wants to knock at the door of our heart, of our own conscience. ***God with us –EMMANUEL–,*** *who wants to befriend us in an incomparable way, a visiting God who wants to come close to our reality. The day I discovered this, I understood that there is no place where Christ cannot come, there is no person, race, skin color, gender, sexual orientation, social, civil, economic condition, that are able to prevent his loving arrival.* God wants you, loves you, understands you, knows your pains and the march you have had on the face of the earth. He knows each of our desires and each of our failures, He knows where we were victorious and where we lost Him, ourselves and our dearest and most beloved ones. God knows our vices, our lies, and yet He wants to find us, because His love is great enough to touch and restore us. His greatest purpose is to touch our weakness to heal us from the fear we have inside to live and overcome.

That is what we were created for, to overcome and be happy, meanwhile, Satan changed our design, convinced us of pride and arrogance and now has us disordered and confused.

God wants to be part of our existence, He made us in His image and likeness. He Himself gave us the beautiful capacity to enjoy free decision. He did not usurp his creative power but wanted to leave us the splendid possibility of being able to decide according to our own capacity to value each of the things, the circumstances. Could there be a love as liberating as God's love? He not only loves creation, but He seeks it with the desire of a creator, He wants to live powerfully with each one of us, He wants to share the freedom of creation itself and to participate in its decisions. *He is truly the Father of fathers, the generous Father, who, while knowing the weakness and fragility of each of his children, wants to accompany them, realizing how difficult it is for them to make the best decisions, to make the most perfect choices, yet he does not take away their freedom, but rather preserves in them their freedom of being.*

During my priestly ministry and later as a Bishop, I have met many people who suffer from insecurity, who are weak in their ability to trust strictly in God. They need human assurances that are not always possible. From this unstable uncertainty of being, many people, from one moment to another, lost themselves in the syndrome of panic, abruptly fell into a very great depression, got inwardly into a moral, emotional, social and physical imprisonment of false scruples, which is nothing more than the deprivation of freedom, not only exterior, but more than anything else, interior. The sick person hides, encloses himself, loses himself in an imaginary world, full of illusory symptoms of helplessness and fear. The sick person loses faith in himself, in the people around him, in the treatments and mediations, loses faith in God. Far from the illumination of faith, far from access to reasonable and healing knowledge, they lose the possibility of a new healing encounter. This whole painful picture reflects how much the person was the victim of direct attacks, not on his faith, not on his capacity for knowledge, but was directly attacked in his freedom. At some point in her life she was trapped by a person, force of emotion or circumstance, which robbed her of her right to be herself in her capacity to decide. God never opposes our decisions, even if they oppose Him. Freedom is the framework of our encounter with God, it must be born from within us, the desire to be and remain in His presence, this is the mysterious communion of love; in which the soul in love gives itself faithfully to the Lord. At this moment faith and knowledge unite in a perennial way to transform this relationship into a miracle of infinite love.

How many deacons, priests, bishops, I have known throughout my life, men of faith, men of prayer life, with multiple gifts, who went through the process of depression. Given the conditions of the difficult times we are living in, the transience of values, the change of the role of people in society to a negative standard, the various economic challenges and the weakening of faith and the values of the spiritual life, many have been severely tested and some have succumbed. Unfortunately I have seen many fall, going through the experience of realizing, sinking in the rough sea, exactly like the apostle Peter when he wanted to walk on the water, when he saw himself sinking he cried out anxiously: "Jesus, save me". Each one must recognize himself in his real condition before Jesus, it is true that we make mistakes and that many times when we think we are strong and stable, in reality we are not. I have seen this happen not only to clergymen, friends of mine, doctors, scientists, academics of great knowledge and great science, teachers, supervisors, managers, self-employed professionals, parents, various types and degrees of people in the most diversified roles, who have also sunk into the traps of uncertainty, insecurity, fear, depression.

Our talents and abilities, however lucid they may be, do not make us immune to the traps. It is increasingly urgent to have clear within oneself the power of faith and the knowledge that we are assisted by God, in order to enjoy the benefits of being kept and guided by his word on a daily basis. It is very important to fight wisely in order to safeguard your freedom, both to believe and to know the different manifestations of God in all your life.

Many people come to our ministry with the desire to seek prayer and find relief in their various difficulties, to them I always address the same question: What are your sins, those that you have refused for years to confess? The reason is because I know that things always have their origin in sins, in doors that we leave open, in wounds that are festering and we are not willing to face them and treat them as they should be. I am sure, in the experience of my ministry, that things that start badly, always end badly.

Many who are good, we learn to love, everything seems wonderful, but if there is something hidden, well camouflaged inside, when you least expect it, no matter how prepared you are, you will be surprised with the impact of the inner novelty that was hidden and this could be the reason for more pain, relationship difficulties or even separation. It does not only happen in churches, communities, work, but in all the different levels of operations between people who relate to each other. If we really want to open ourselves to one another, this process must begin by really opening ourselves totally before Christ. It does not matter who we were, where we have come from for judgmental census, but it is highly important to create trust and true willingness to help each other without prejudice and judgment, loving each other and recognizing in each other the potential necessary to excel.

With all my heart, with all my faith and all the instruments and tools offered by God as favorable talents to the edification of the people in the faith, I have given myself to the service of all. As a faithful worker and servant of the gospel, I have put all the service, not in broken sacks, but all that I have consecrated with love and sacrifice, is in the hands of God. I have worked with the immense ardor of a shepherd, I have sought the effective means to bring all those who are willing to grow in faith and in the knowledge of the grace of God. This is the goal and for it I strive day after day.

VIII. The Unexpected Encounter

*"And ye shall seek me and find me,
for you will seek me with all your heart".* Jeremiah 29:13.

"**B**lessed and praised be the Lord, this day of today I thank you, Lord God. You are good, infinitely good. Your mercy is everlasting. Your glory is ineffably the source of all good things and of all graces. I want to bless you Lord, for the gift of our lives, especially for all the graces, because with such generous and true affection, you touch each one of our lives. Thank you Lord, because your hands touch our hearts to fill each one of us with the necessary blessings. Thank you Lord because you destine your mercy for us, because in our lives we have the sign of your powerful hands, for sustaining us, especially me, your beloved son. If your favors were not to keep us, what would have become of my life? If you were not searching my heart and teaching me through visible signs of your mighty strength, I would not be able to understand the importance of living the virtue of grace that emanates from your mercy. I adore you Lord. I bless you because every day you purify me with your providence. Thank you Lord because every day you renew with me the agreement of the covenant of blessing. Thank you Lord because you make me enter the hidden refuge of your great presence to praise you, to bless you. I want to unite myself in communion of faith with all the people who are receiving the power of this prayer, the power of this intercession. I want to bring here all the people who are longing for a great miracle at this hour, a great blessing to those who are crying out to you Lord, perhaps with tears. We invoke you with love through the intercessory power of your most precious blood.

Come Jesus Divine Master, who receives each and every one of us in your presence. Cleanse from our hearts all filthiness, all that turns us away and prevents us from adoring your glorious presence, your divine majesty. Cleanse us from the vices and inner wounds that do not allow us to open ourselves totally to your immense power. Heal, Lord, the scourges. Heal the wounds, the lashes that we have received from unjust and ungodly hands. Lord, you are a good and true friend. I know that you take care of each one of us. You know exactly Lord, all the damages and difficulties that we are living and going through. You have counted the losses that we have had. You know Lord each one of our weaknesses, of our falls, of our failures. You have in your blessed powerful hands, the ineffable power of your *divine will to take us and that is why we cry Lord. Come to our aid in this hour. Do not leave us at the mercy of those who persecute us. Extend your hand and bless us with your protection.*

Your greatness is incomparable. You are great Lord almighty, not to destroy us or placate us, but your greatness is to embrace our littleness and restore to each of us real dignity. Place each of us in the royal refuge of your love. You are Lord, the generous Father, the one who waits for the son who wants to return. You are the one who is willing to put a new ring on the finger of the son who returns home. You are the one who is willing to offer a new tunic, new sandals. You are the one who is willing to prepare the banquet and choose for the feast the best there is, because we were dead and we are alive again. We were lost and we find ourselves in you. You are the one who restores and celebrates our dignity as children of God. We were lost and you found us. Blessed and praised are you. (Prayer in tongues in the Holy Spirit). "Blessed and praised be you Lord. Strengthen us. Strengthen us with the power that comes from your divine presence. I ask you in this hour that my soul, my intellect, my capacity and inner faculty, be reached by your ineffable greatness. Clothe me, Lord, with the knowledge that flows from you for the education of my brothers in faith and in grace. Especially draw near to me, to be the wisdom that comes from the high heavens. Inspire me and direct me according to your desire. Nourish now Lord my cells, my neurons, every atom of my brain. Fill me with the most precious blood of our Lord Jesus Christ, with the purifying water that came down from the open side of Jesus on the cross, so that I may be healed. Take Lord my voice, all my sonorous devices. Take Lord my tongue. I consecrate my whole being to your service. Use me, Divine Master. (Prayer in tongues in the Holy Spirit). All my body, all my soul, my spirit, that are susceptible, now to your word breathe. Blessed are you Lord".

In this spiritual journey that we are making, we are discovering the existence of the fear that we latently have of finding and being found. Life in God is something so expressive, marvelous, enchanting, that for a moment we want to be like Peter, James and John, stunned, alone, without coming down from Mount Tabor. Jesus invites them to come down, to abandon the ideals of faith drawn in their minds from their spiritual desires. Jesus shows them the way back, gives them the direct command that makes them go out to meet the others who were down in the valley.

Every encounter in our existence is intimately marked by the power of feeling, whether called sympathy or antipathy. All mankind seems to fight with itself, ardently desiring only empathic encounters, positive interpellations, loves at first sight. All this sounds nice. It is music to the ears, but it is not reality. Things do not work at this pace and in this way. Each encounter is more than the reception of what is pleasurable, because everything that is pleasurable ends up being sometimes passion-ate. What pleases me today, now, may cease to exert its effectiveness tomorrow or in the following moments. It is supremely important when the encounter allows me to contemplate the focus of the encounter, when it allows me to find meaning and census of value. The encounter takes on new dimensions when it exceeds the primary expectations, when it surprises us with possible new perspectives and challenges us in a forceful way to ponder and evaluate what is truly good, praiseworthy and acceptable to the aggrandizement of oneself and of the moment.

Many people end up making their possibilities of encounters, reasons for pity, because if one only wants to meet what pleases him, he will easily be disappointed. The many failed attempts most of the time lead people to isolate themselves. It is much more difficult to find someone who pleases us than to find someone who easily turns into disaffection. The secret of true encounter lies in the ability to accept being disappointed by the other without so many prejudices or false expectations. The en-counter will always be a great possibility to experience the new and the different and thus find something that will allow us to grow and learn. That is why Jesus, when speaking to his apostles and disciples, as when speaking to the Pharisees, insisted em-phatically in repeating: *"I did not come to find the healthy to heal them, I came to find the sick to restore them to health" (Mark 2:17)*. Jesus definitely did not expect to meet with the righteous, but with sinners, with the most despised of his time. If Jesus wanted to meet with the rulers, Jesus would not have been able to fulfill the mission of the Father. *The true encounter is revealed when we are able to leave the comfortable environment of our existence, of our capacities, of our zones of control and domination, when we are able to leave all that is in us and renounce all that makes us feel that we are superior in order to go towards what is different and apparently challenging and uncomfortable. This is the path taken and chosen for Jesus' encounters while he was among us.*

When someone decides to leave this area easily inhabited by himself to go into the unknown, into the universe of others and to be able to offer himself as an ac-ceptable person, without fear, without prejudice, without condemnation, without privileges and advantages, is when he will truly be confronting face to face the great challenge of finding and being found.

True encounters happen when we decide to make ourselves available to be a person, to present ourselves as we are. If we look at the children playing on the beach or in the garden of our homes or schools, we will see them free of pretense, each one giving himself as he is. When we observe how they relate to each other, we will understand what I have just written. Children are given encounters free of any pre-existing prejudices of race, ethnicity, social level. None of this is import-

ant. They are not afraid of each other. They just want to share and discover togeth-er. God taught me to admire the nobility and purity of children and learn from them to be a better person. They are not concerned with nationalities, languages, or clothes. They are just open to meeting new people and learning. Everything for them is centered on the joy of meeting. They hug. They share toys. They sit down to play. They make castles. They destroy castles. The friendship remains there fault-lessly real until the parents decide to separate them and every child carries within himself the sure longing for a possible reunion. Who does not miss his childhood friends? How much would we give to go back to the same places, with the first com-panions with whom we played? It would definitely be a wonderful thing.

Jesus wanted to preserve the freedom and protection of children and he himself said: *"Let the little children come to me, for to them belongs the kingdom of heav-en" (Matthew 19:14).* The whole secret of our life lies in recognizing the power and efficacy that exist in the magnificent encounter with Christ. The man who wants to be happy, the man who truly seeks happiness, will never achieve his purpose and will never be able to live abundantly unless he first learns the privilege of enjoying the experience of the encounter with Christ.

The encounter with himself, the real and true encounter with those who are part of his history and definitely the encounter with God. The entire ministry of Jesus, the Galilean Nazarene, is revealed at the moment when he begins his public life and be-gins to walk from city to city and meet with different situations and people. At each step of the Galilean Nazarene, the focus was centered on the opportunity to meet with each of the people who presented themselves along the way. Naturally, Jesus was born with the faithful intention of offering them the possibility of change, of trans-forming the occasion of that approach into a potential occasion of a true miraculous encounter. The encounter was for Jesus the means to allow him to bring them closer to transformation and restoration. Jesus did not invent new laws, he did not create new public bodies, he only began to walk and to let himself be encountered. He al-lowed himself to give himself and to open himself to the encounter with the people most in need of his presence.

I would like to remind you of Jesus' encounter with the hemorrhaging woman. She left her house with an intense desire to touch Jesus. She knew she was going to be challenged by a large crowd of people following him. She knew her uncomfort-able health condition she brought. She was aware of the obstacles she would have to overcome to be as close as possible to that great man, Jesus the Divine Nazarene. He was the true reason for that humble woman's desire to meet him. She thought: *"If only I could touch the hem of his garments, it would be enough for me to be healed" (Matthew 9:21).* So her heart was filled with this immeasurable desire for the moment when it would be possible for her to enjoy the privilege of the encounter with Jesus.

Just as she desired, so it was fulfilled. She was able to touch the border of the garment, of the sacred mantle of Jesus. The woman did not cry out. She did not express any manifestation, simply the touch of faith through her hands. Immediately the force, the power, the energy that existed in the desire of the encounter between her and Jesus, made something move in the bowels of the Divine Master. Jesus felt, perceived the dynamic movement within him. He realized that someone had touched him and Peter said: *"Of course Lord, someone touched you, we are surrounded by people on all sides", but Jesus replied: "Yes Peter, but someone touched me in a different way".*

The encounter, whether scheduled or casual, will never cease to be the space for us to act in a different way. Therein lies the focus of Jesus› encounter with the hemorrhaging woman. She touched in a different way.

It is becoming more and more necessary for us to go out of our commonplace, in order to abandon definitively our realities dominated by ourselves. Each encounter must be unique and unrepeatable. Since it will always be unique, it is impossible to think of repeating what has already been lived. Each experience is new and each encounter is a possibility we have to discover something different. Many people tell me: "Every Mass with you, Monsignor, is different". I am glad and that is how it should be. Each encounter with the Lord should touch us in a new way, to the point of making us fall more and more in love with his presence. One day I learned that one encounter prepares the other and thus all are surprisingly new and unforgettable. Each encounter is unique and particular. It is like someone who jumps in a river of running water. He can jump 10 times and will never jump in the same water, because the river flows and the waters are renewed. In the same way life renews itself. The life of each one of us also changes dynamically and with it our way of being and thinking. Every day we become different people. Each encounter is a unique opportunity. We have to find the difference, the novelty exposed through the other, not to separate us or to exclude us from someone for any reason whatsoever, but so that we learn to contemplate the beauty of the new and the power of creation, the creativity with which we present ourselves and the power of our abilities to surpass ourselves and make ourselves attractive. All this pleasant potential, serves to unite us to the mystery of our lives to learn, to live a little of the other to whom God brings us closer. It is the experience of letting something powerful come out of us, which enables the other to be renewed and also to allow us to receive in us the potential of others. It is a magnificent communion of love.

At that moment Jesus could have continued walking, but he wanted to stop. He stopped in the middle of the crowd and began to look for the one who had touched him. Whoever wants to find someone must learn to get out of the commotion in order to pay real attention. No one can find someone in the midst of disorder. There are no encounters in the midst of haste; it is a real part of the encounter to look, to discover, to feel, to listen, to converse. The encounter in us is the living manifestation of the power of love.

Jesus felt that virtue had gone out of him. Every time we meet a person, every time we talk to someone, every time we are willing to open ourselves to one another through the grace of God, through faith, through the testimony of love, virtue comes out of us. This is and should continue to be the differential of the people of God in this existence. We are called to reflect the virtue of understanding, of esteem, of consolation, of commiseration, the virtue of forgiveness, the virtue of humility, the virtue of compassion, the virtue of faith, the virtue of respect, the virtue of acceptance. When we are truly willing to throw ourselves into this powerful sea of communion, we discover that the encounter is more than mere communication or exchange of information and experiences. We realize that every encounter is more than mere formalism. We perceive that every encounter is embodied in the loving mystery of God who invites us to make it grow, multiply and expand the presence of God in ourselves and in those with whom he allows us to meet.

For the meeting to be fully effective, there must be a real decision on the part of the parties involved. It must contain real desires for closeness, reflection and learning. When I refer to desires, I am not referring to perishable desires that violate the freedom of others. I am talking about desires that are born of virtues, of joy, of receptivity, of the simplicity of really wanting to welcome the new. Mostly, the human being itself. When it comes to us, we are fleeting and weak. Many of us seek advantages and with this vulnerability we can easily damage the preciousness of the encounter. If there is not the quality of respect and the decision to build on solid values, the encounters become vulgar because they are motivated by weak desires, fragile of true feelings and become only momentary. When we really meet a fellow human being and we want lasting love to be born from this encounter, we must see in the other the sign of Christ, the presence of Christ, even if the person is in a situation lacking in favorable privileges. No one should despise the possibility of finding in the other, no matter how invisible, the divine vision of grace. Throughout my life, the greatest gifts have come from people I could never expect. People sent to meet me by the Lord himself, so I learned to love without barriers or prejudice. I met very victimized failed people. I learned from them. I received much more than I could offer. It was part of the mystery of the encounter through the love of God. There in them, among us, was Jesus. As he himself taught us: *"When I was hungry you fed me, when I was thirsty you gave me a drink, when I was a stranger in the street you gave me a house and shelter, when I was sick you took care of me, when I was in prison you came to visit me".* Then they asked him: *"When was it that we saw you like this? (Matthew 25:35-36),* and the Lord, in all wisdom, answered them, *"All the times you have failed to find me, hidden in the heart of the most wretched who needed an encounter to find peace and salvation."*

When I discovered the real meaning of this part of the gospel of our Lord Jesus Christ, I felt a deep shame of myself and of all the encounters that could have been sources of miracles and by my ignorance I had spoiled them. No doubt it pained me to realize that I had let my Lord down, for all the times that I judged, that I condemned arbitrarily, that I did not pay real attention to those who came to me. They were in an unfavorable situation. Sometimes I made them inferior to my time, because of much to do, for other people without allowing me to see and recognize Jesus hidden in each one of them. It is time that we open ourselves to the perception that Jesus Christ asks for shelter, asks to meet us in the most different ways, forms and persons. He wants to pass through, he wants to awaken in our hearts the possibility of encountering the powerful virtue that comes from him.

IX. The Power of the Beatitude

"Blessed are the pure in heart,
for they shall see God". Matthew 5:8-10.

Even talking about the encounter, we know that he has the power to change a person's history. He has the dynamic authority. He can even destroy it totally. It all depends on the powerful force and the intervention of the person or persons involved in the encounter itself. It is my purpose now to tell you about Jesus' encounter with Zacchaeus, *the tax collector*. He was perplexed by all the things he had heard about Jesus. He had within himself a deep desire to see him, just to see him. That would be enough for him. He wanted to see Jesus to probe the Lord's attitudes. Zacchaeus was eager to evaluate and understand if what he had heard about the Nazarene really agreed with what he was about to see. He wanted to know Jesus' procedure. His great impact was not only what he saw in Jesus. The encounter was not one-sided and based only on Zacchaeus' perspective. Jesus also looked at him at the top of the tree. Jesus, in looking at him, also wanted that encounter to be more profound than a simple exchange of glances. Jesus addressed him saying: "Come down Zacchaeus, come down. You do not need to look at me from afar, we can come closer". This is the most effective suggestion for the encounter, to look face to face, to contemplate from person to person, without creating obstacles of difference, but only giving each other the opportunity to offer each other the necessary respect and the possibility of the miracle. Jesus said to Zacchaeus: "Today I will dine at your house". These are recurring realities of the encounter. The encounter is not defined or enclosed in itself, but the true encounter, moved and guided by the grace of God, by the power of the Holy Spirit, by the strength of the love of our Lord Jesus Christ, brings in itself a redemptive meaning. This encounter will then be able to propel us to greater and greater things.

Zacchaeus understood the call. He perceived the dimension of the significance of that self-invitation of Jesus. He immediately waited for the master to come to his house for dinner. He began to prepare the environment and also to prepare himself in his conscience. *The true encounters always stand out for the possibility of other encounters. The encounters are not enclosed within themselves, but they are capable of opening doors never imagined, opportunities never thought of and graces never expected. Every encounter, moved and oriented by the grace of God, does not look only at the number, conditions, status, origins of the people. The encounter is the means, the network, the instruments necessary for God to begin to work in us the miracle of his fulfilling presence. That is to say, every encounter in God is full of manifestations that will bring about real changes involving the whole dimensions of those who meet. For that reason Jesus said: "Where two or three are gathered in my name, I am in their midst". (Matthew 18:20).*

When we meet, it is not only we who are happy. Every encounter that brings Christ as mediator accurately reflects the powerful beauty of the grace contained in his love. Certainly this encounter manifests God through our lives. The spaces are diminished in order that the virtue of communion may be realized in us. Jesus arrived at Zacchaeus' house and now it is Zacchaeus' attitude that will speak loudly. He receives him with all the love of his heart, but without hiding his reality. The unjust tax collector, Zacchaeus himself does not mask his reality, but recognizes that he had sinned a lot. He recognizes his debts and crimes. But he knew that everything that had happened did not prevent him from changing his life after that first encounter with the master.

For sure, Jesus, who had looked Zacchaeus in the eyes and had truly probed all his dispositions, said aloud: *"Today salvation has come to this house" (Luke 19:1-10)*. It was not the mere fact of Jesus' arrival, but it was salvation through the complete rescue of that person. There was an encounter based on love, on truth and life itself gave him the opportunity to open up, repent and be rehabilitated. It was not only a social encounter of Jesus with Zacchaeus, it was the encounter of the repentant sinner with the savior full of love and mercy with the desire to love. It was the encounter of saving grace. Salvation itself with the repentant and penitent attitude expressed in the attitudes of Zacchaeus, this is a true encounter.

Not only the arrival of the things that come, but also the real reception of the things that come with all their potential of challenges and changes. That is why the word encounter means the union of all, of two strong sides for the composition of a single thing, reality and communication of diverse shades and values, but with well-defined objectives for the general good. There will be no encounter if there is no unity. There is no unity if there is no way to grow together. It is not possible to grow together if the powerful force of love, forgiveness and connection does not prevail among the related ones.

Jesus' arrival at Zacchaeus' house caused him to change his way of being and acting. In this encounter of Jesus with Zacchaeus there is a direct interference in the ethics and character of that man. He assumes a new moral condition, abandons his vices and assumes from then on an exact manner of one who has found salvation, which is a new and great meaning for his life. He who has found salvation no longer needs usury, abuse, usurpation and definitely nothing that is superfluous or the fruit of theft or injustice. Zacchaeus understood that, on that day, from that encounter, salvation had come into his heart. He discovered a new value for his life and his actions. He received the necessary virtue to free him from everything that had enslaved and trapped him. He was freed from the prison of attachments and lies about material goods.

The encounter between Jesus and Zacchaeus does not only change the life of the tax collector, but it also directly changes in visible consequences the environment of the other people who were under the mercy of Zacchaeus and who had been exploited by their former condition of life. These people also received salvation and the benefits of grace descended from it. Each was to receive back that which had been unjustly taken from them.

When someone is willing to open their heart to another person, not just help, grace will be abundant for all related to both people. The good that is shared with love and justice, nourished by truth and virtues, will consequently reach other people, to an extent never before imagined. *Every encounter in Christ and through Christ is the real bearer of a powerful force of restoration and renewal. When we allow ourselves to be found in the presence of God, our life assumes the character of being a faithful bearer of love and our living is also allowed to be a source of blessing for our relatives, our friends, for the people directly and indirectly linked to the course of our existence.*

My question is the following: *why then so many models, so many paradigms, why then so much laziness, so much lack of development and personal commitment to widen the spaces of our encounters and to transform the origin of our relationships?*

Many people come to talk to me and many of them share with me their anxieties and fears, their inner confusions and end up asking: what do I have to offer to another person? I feel like such a poor person... I have been impoverished throughout my life. Almost everything has been taken away from me. I do not feel pleasure in going out and meeting people. I do not feel pleasure in talking to anyone. I see life as gray. Everything is heavy, difficult, everything makes me feel afraid to isolate myself. I clearly perceive that I have innumerable barriers. I feel that people judge me and avoid me because of my unstable character and mood. I think that I do not make myself understood when I speak. I think that I do not know how to explain my actions and feelings. All this perhaps because I have not understood myself.

As you are thinking, it is a very difficult terrain to walk on. It takes a lot of work to disrupt so many states of enchainment and low self-esteem. It is necessary to be willing to advance towards the first causes that disordered, not only some isolated actions of the person in himself, but to touch deeper realities that are blocking the whole existence of the person.

Immediately, the first thing I do is look them in the eye, give them a smile of faith. With deep respect and pastoral attitude, I extend my hand to them, tell them: "Don't be in a hurry. Accept giving today to your life, to yourself and to God, a unique opportunity. Everything can be changed through a change of view". Just like the man in the field who begins to enter a closed forest, I begin little by little to find the space to become closer to that person and his soul. Until I can reach the space, the precise place, the memory, the feeling, the memory still sometimes confused by the destabilizing circumstances, perhaps to find a detail or a kind of conversation where the person begins to open decisively to the inner healing and liberation. It takes great love for Christ, immense faith and integrity of character to be willing to engage in this work of inner healing through real and very hurtful events.

To bring it all out and expose it to the outside, is a work of deep healing. Going back to past realities is often horrible, painful and demanding, but until today it has been the most effective way to truly free yourself and take on a new life. The healing encounter is truly unforgettable. God works directly and exclusively through the one who is left to not only cleanse, but totally restore lives. As a minister of grace, a pastor of God's work and an instrument of our Lord Jesus Christ, I am overwhelmed by so much love and beauty reflected in the manifestation of God. It is wonderful to see how God takes us without us having the minimum human and scientific preparation or strategy. It is God himself who intervenes through his healing love and directs us to the exact place, to the specific situation, where the focus is, the origin of the maladjustment and disease. He guides us to the necessary reality of light, spiritual education, blessing, healing and restoration. My task is to do nothing more than to open the doors so that Christ Himself can enter and work in each person. All merit and glory to the Lord, honor, glory, praise for the ages without end.

When I talk about this I feel like crying. My heart is moved and my mind is not able to enumerate and remember exactly all the people that God has allowed me to meet throughout my life, and to supply them with inner healing. There were many retreats, meetings, seminars, preaching, mornings, afternoons, evenings, nights, healing vigils for hundreds of people. Prayer groups, healing masses, in short, many trips, different countries, cultures, but always the Lord teaching me that the work does not end and that we must offer everything for the salvation, healing, liberation and sanctification of a soul through love. If I could count or remember names, it would not have been the Lord, but I would have been responsible for so many blessings. God is the God of wonders. He uses us even when we do not perceive it.

Each encounter with Jesus Christ is unique and unrepeatable. Sometimes I want to repeat advice to a person that I had already given to another and it is the Holy Spirit Himself who comes, takes my mind and changes everything. Each manifestation of God in our lives is unique in order to make each person be touched in a personal and unmistakable way. Precisely because each person is unique, the stories are similar and sometimes confusing, but each being is unique and assimilates differently, each heart feels in its own way.

In the face of such a diverse universe, it is necessary to look at each person in his or her individuality in order to understand and love him or her as required. It is not possible to try to help someone relatively subjective. Our actions must be submissive to the continuous action of God's will. Helping a person demands from the one who submits to such a demanding action, a fine and dense relationship with the will of God. We must be obedient and learn to reveal God's will and our own particular conceptions. That is why many parents, pastors, even fathers of families, cause much damage, because they want to act leading people under their own morals and way of thinking. To form a soul and lead a person to progress as an individual, as a whole person, integral and honest, requires from the actors in this process, a deep spiritual coherence and life of intimacy with God.

Do not shut yourself up in your egoism. Do not shut yourself up in those ideas that isolate you from reality. Do not shut yourself up behind emotional masks and fantasies. Do not shut yourself up behind the screens of cell phones, computers. Do not shut yourself up behind your obligations. Don't lock yourself behind the curtains of fear and shame that are in the windows of your soul. Don't lock yourself in the isolated shortcuts that suggest disorder and loss of values. Don't lock yourself in the infinite needs that don't allow you to get anywhere.

Open yourself. Ephphet, means open. Open your heart. Open your soul. Open your mind. Open your spirit so that you can contemplate what lies beyond the horizon. Every person who is truly open, can make the transcendental experience of faith and thus be able to look with spiritual eyes, through the light that comes from the high heavens, to see concretely through Jesus. Open yourself. It is the opportune time for you to come out of this manipulative capsule that does not allow you to be yourself fully. Open yourself. Go out like the caterpillar that struggles arduously to overcome itself, until it breaks all the physical and natural barriers to transform itself into a dragonfly, into a beautiful butterfly. Open yourself in a healthy way to illuminate. Open yourself to reflect, through you, the powerful force of God capable of touching others.

Sometimes some people ask me: what do you have? How do you become the way you are? Humanly speaking, I am an ordinary man, full of defects that must be healed every day, but this strength, this faith, this authority, these gifts, charisms, abilities, capacities, all this does not belong to me. It is all God's grace. I have nothing of myself that is not my own freedom in assuming or not assuming the gift of God. Everything that I experience is from God. It comes from God. I have received everything freely because I have opened myself to the Lord, to whom I consecrated my whole being and it was through the many falls and ups and downs that the Lord was educating my mind, my heart, my soul, my intellect to live at his disposal, at the service of the gospel in the church, the body of Christ. One day, sensibly, I gave myself to Jesus without imagining all that this would imply. I was just a child. He accepted me, took my word seriously and from then on, we began a beautiful story of love encounters.

Open yourself. I know that you must have some problem, some great need you must be going through at this moment. The secret is not to shut yourself up in your own, and perhaps confused thoughts. Don't think you are automatically capable. Don't feel self sufficient. Look for help. God has someone there. Next to you there is a person waiting for the opportunity to meet you. Very close to you God is preparing a person to be the possibility of a miracle in your existence.

Through my experience I want to teach you. God is teaching me. His love is revealing to me to share with you and tell you, to call your attention to the desire that you be able to love without prejudice. *"God hid wisdom from the wise of this world, because he wanted to reveal it to the humble." (Matthew 11:25).* His infinite goodness, generosity and merciful love, despise no one. I am sure that the word of solution that you need, this important answer that you are waiting for, can come at any moment. It will come through the one you least expect. Even you have been looking for it but unable to find it on your own. Don't worry, God is at work. The Holy Spirit blows where He wills. God will prepare the encounter with the instrument that will bring you peace, comfort, response and blessing.

Give it a try. Let God act. Let the Holy Spirit send whomever He wills, and in whatever way He wills. Hallelujah. Let your life under God's movement, learn to surrender everything into His hands.

As you are now, I invite you to enter into prayer.

God, I thank you for all my brothers and especially for this person who is here now in prayer with me. Before God I bless you, receive your mission, leave decisively today the idleness, the emptiness in being selfish, greedy, leave, for love of God and the desire for change, all ties of revenge, stop oppressing and rancor to bring some people tied within their feelings of hatred and enmity. Make a commitment today to ask God for forgiveness from your heart. Open your heart so that you can love and receive each person within your heart. Learn to forgive them with humility and generosity. Be willing to open your formerly closed arms and, like Jesus himself, reject no one. Blessed of God, follow with faith every advice present in this prayer. It is for you an opportunity to open yourself to divine encounters, to spiritual encounters, to encounters that are born directly from the will and grace of God. Do not be discouraged, God is with you. God is with us.

It is also very important to speak of the beautiful encounter of Jesus when, on the mountains, he looked at the city of Jerusalem and said: *"Jerusalem, Jerusalem, you who kill the prophets and stone those who were sent to you, how often I wanted to gather your children together as a hen gathers her chicks under her wings, but you rejected me."* Jesus teaches us, through this word, to understand that not all desired encounters are possible. Undoubtedly there is something horrible called rejection. A kind of masked feeling of pride and self-sufficiency that has crept into humanity, capable of damaging any possibility of closeness to the other in a real and forceful way. Incoherent rejection is an evil action capable of damaging free will, leading our freedom to rebellion and thus confusing our decisions and deliberations.

How many people come to me saying: "I wanted to do it, I wanted to be, I wanted to be, I wanted to commit myself, but something paralyzed me, pulled me back". That something is called rejection. That something is this lazy weakness that settles inside us, that easily acts and discourages us, takes away our focus, destabilizes us emotionally. Rejection as a selfish and ignorant act of truth, is a symptom of the rebelliousness of people who wish to remain oblivious to truth and light, people who deny themselves the opportunity for change, situations and conditions that prefer isolation rather than fraternity and love. It is the reflection of people who only value the perspective seen from the outside of themselves, of those who do not want to give themselves the opportunity of an inward journey that will lead them to a much more effective well-being.

Jesus looked at Jerusalem and Jesus saw in the city of Jerusalem its potential as the Holy City of God. She would be very different if it were not for her pride, if it were not for her misery of human values, if it were not for her hypocrisy, if it were not for her many unnecessary interests. Jesus wanted to cherish Jerusalem, but Jerusalem wanted to kill him. Desires totally opposed to each other, very similar to the present times. The same city of Jerusalem that on Sunday received him saying: Hosanna the son of David! A week later it would reject him shouting: Barabbas, Barabbas, Barabbas, crucify him, crucify Jesus and release Barabbas! This same Jerusalem that came to him on Sunday with green palms and cloaks that they threw along the road so that the King, son of David, would pass, was the same Jerusalem that a few days later would throw stones, blows and shouts of insults at him.

Many times we are ready to give everything for an encounter capable of helping someone, to do something favorable, to raise possibilities of rescuing the person offering him means to become a new person, to open the field to offer him a different opportunity of life and not everything is given. We realize that there is no positive response that allows us to help. On the other side there is only silence, indifference, apathy and rejection. Jesus wants to embrace you. Jesus wants to keep you warm. Jesus wants to bring to you the powerful force of his love. Let him give you all his favors. Do not put yourself aside from this wonderful opportunity. Do it for you, to be a better person, to live with quality, to offer to those who love you, the joy of your change and healing. Someone wants to ask you for forgiveness, but you keep rejecting. Someone wants to approach you and tells you they want to change, but you don't believe it and keep rejecting. Someone wants to tell you that things will be different, but you don't allow yourself to believe in the new because you are stuck in the past of mistakes.

X. The Encounter, Path of Justice and Inner Healing

"Seek first the kingdom of God and his righteousness." Matthew 6:31.

The essence of an encounter is the simplest traces that he himself leaves in us. They are the signs, lights, effects, wonders, teachings and feelings that awaken within us. Each encounter enlightens our being with new knowledge and gives us the possibility of building bridges of access, if we are truly humble and capable of pursuing the gloriousness of God revealed with powerful force in our daily lives.

To seek the kingdom of God is to follow Christ, to focus on his word, to discover the power of his presence, to surrender and be truly converted by his love. The love of Jesus is what gloriously drives our saving redemption. This is the central profile of an authentic encounter formatted through mercy in love.

Every opportunity for encounter is a grace we experience directly provided by the hands of God himself. He did not create us to dwell in solitude; his purpose from the beginning was our freedom, happiness, fulfillment and an existence of communion. He formed us through his generosity so that in it we would learn to love and discover the love shared with justice in every creature in creation.

When we allow our being to encounter God, something wonderfully great and powerful happens causing the immediate extension of this relationship offering peace to the earth, we are filled with his love revealed in Christ Jesus, we soberly allow ourselves to enjoy the satisfying blow of the Holy Spirit.

The encounter under the power of the Holy Spirit opens for us the prospect of a fruitful and fertile happiness and we can then experience the gifts and charisms. Living this blissful communion and receiving these gifts focuses us on the most essential and principal of our mission to ourselves, to those closest to us, to those far away, to the universe in its fullness. The gifts and charisms well lived and shared free us from fears, chains of traumas, traces of accusations from the past aged by sin, free us from isolation and a life of hiding.

This encounter is liberating and comfortable, effectively capable of transporting us to newness of intimate and external life *(2 Corinthians 5:17)*, if we assume to live from the goal of faith, in being a new child restored in love, forgiven of its sins, renewed in faith, strengthened in its works and contemplated among men and women of good will. Let us pray in faith:

"Lord, my God, I beseech you that you could reach the simplest part of each person, of each heart, ask you in this hour Lord, that your Holy Spirit may move each one towards the truth of the knowledge of your love and they may be, not only touched from the point of view of the ability to understand, but that they may be touched by the power of the goodness that you communicate to us from your love. May their eyes be opened, their senses be awakened, their capacity and availability be worked and elaborated towards the service of the common good. We entrust to you, Lord, their lives, that they may truly be healed of ignorance and all kinds of rejection of your love. May they be awakened so that they may understand the need to give a concrete witness to the people closest to them, to the people who need to make a change in their lives, to the people who are waiting for a special grace, a decisive miracle. This is the time Lord, the time of the manifestation of your Holy Spirit, so that the grace of this New Pentecost may enlighten us to work for the approach of all people to your throne of grace and blessing".

Being together does not basically mean a real encounter. Living together, sharing the same physical, material and corporate space is not synonymous with encounter. The fact of developing joint tasks is not yet understood as an effective encounter. Many times we are together, we develop tasks together, however, our souls, our feelings, desires and searches, do not flow towards the same thing. The atmosphere is marked by rivalries, competitions, disputes and mental and material divisions. The fact that we are together and the fact that we share the same place does not mean that we have the same heart, the same desire. It is as if we were in a photo, all hugged, together, smiling very easily, but behind the photo there is another existing reality. We find that reality reflected in our families, they are all within the same inheritance of blood and values, but the prerogatives and events in most of the times run each one on their own path. Maybe that is why many of us have not yet been able to find in our families our own place, our own objective identification, because we lack the encounter between our closest ones, we are together, but we are not united supporting each other as we should through the feelings and actions of the family.

Some people come to talk to me and ask me: how can I find my place within my family? I feel as if that family is not mine, as if I am not part of them, I feel alien to everyone and everything that concerns my family.

When we are isolated from the bond of love, this usually happens, especially when we just share roof, food and house, it is different when we share home, family and communion. It is time for us to be able to recognize that where we are, we are not there because we choose to be. The family reflects God's will for each one of us, God gave us this mark and put us where we are, not so that we destroy ourselves, but so that we learn to develop noble and authentic values based on love.

To learn to love, to accept, to embrace and to love starting from where we are, to understand our origin, where we come from, to understand that God put us there with a real objective; not just so that we would only occupy the same temporal, physical and material space, but God constituted us in families so that we would share the essence and the mystery, the specific mission to be shared with these people, in these scarce or favorable conditions.

The family, among its members, is unfortunately full of jealousy; how many homes I know and hear from its members the complaints that they kill and fight over little things. The family allowed to develop in its bosom the massive pride, causing among its members many wounds, resentments, grudges and endless discord. Prejudices, unnecessary criticisms and judgments are born from the bosom of the family itself. Among the family members themselves, they take care of separating and devaluing each other. It is visible to perceive the lack of understanding of some in relation to others.

We still find in the family the presence of ties of revenge, of excessive hatred. How sad it all is, the family is still full of deceptions, frauds, betrayals, corrupt actions that undermine the possibility of loving each other and sharing the sense of being part of this family.

How is it possible to survive in a house with such a sandy ground? How is it possible to sustain a family in an environment of so many rivalries and differences? Parents misaligned, sunk in blind selfishness, parents divided among themselves, the presence of so many vices, irresponsibility. Spiteful and abusive parents who have denied the real power of forgiveness. Defrauded children and I am sure that this is the most painful thing at the heart of the family. Children who suffer and pay for the maladjustment of their parents, for the ignorance of those who are absorbed in their own miseries and do not realize the destruction of the home. Parents have forgotten and prefer to put aside the possibility of understanding their primary mission, to form a family and establish the dwelling of God in the home. I always talk to the children who with me vent their hopes for answers. They keep waiting and longing for love, they expect affection, they expect attention to their dilemmas. They come forward to ask questions and share their experiences, they seek healing. It is because of these situations and troubled environments that so many misfortunes are happening. The children are frustrated and end up looking outside, in false friendships, in vices, in mental laziness, in irreverent irresponsibility, for their secure support. Many children are in deep depression, victims of their own families. Many are more and more submissive to their weak illusions that will only bring more pain and more family and social dislocation.

How many young people I see in the streets, many times I stop the car and look at them in the parks, and they are suffering. Others in the alleys using marijuana pipes and other hallucinogens. I ask myself: Where is the family? Where are the parents? Maybe they are lost in their own things, in their unnecessary illusions, in the pursuit of things that will never end, in the chore of things that every day will multiply more and more. While all this is going on, their children are becoming more and more distant and isolated. Many children are being tormented by deep sadness, inside their own homes, in their rooms, which they want to paint black, without light, many barely want to sleep, others start cutting their arm, their legs with razors, others paint demons and strange faces, frightening things.

There is a rush in the world, but people do not walk towards a peaceful encounter, unhappily, the great mass of people walk towards disarrangement, towards the misunderstanding of themselves. More than ever it seems to me that humanity is in a hurry and eager to fill itself with things that are not really fulfilling, they are desperate to fill themselves with events that, at the moment of truth, are of no use to them. *Throughout my ministry I have learned that if the family is not well, if the family is not united, all the goods and values will easily disappear. If there is no love, understanding, comprehension and mutual support, nothing, no action will have any effectiveness. It is necessary in this time in which we are struggling with all that, to assume the baptismal call to be king, priest and prophet. I recognize that the Lord has called me, the Lord has enlightened me, the Lord has put words on my lips to prophesy to you, to your homes, to your children. The Gospel especially tells us: "The Spirit of the Lord is upon me to preach good news to the poor, to heal the brokenhearted, to proclaim release to those who are in chains, to restore sight to the blind, deliverance to all who are oppressed, and to proclaim the time of the Lord's favor" (Luke 4:18-19).* In mentioning and sharing deeply with you on the subject of the priority need for an encounter, I am speaking to you exactly about this very scarce time of this reality. We need each one of us to be open to the real possibility of a rebirth, a revival of faith, a renewal of mind and values, a structural change of vital emphasis, in order to come out of the darkness and move towards the light. If this change does not happen in a decisive and radical way, the challenges will continue to become more and more uncontrollable. Do you want to analyze this reality, get out of the window and go inside your own home, I invite you to think and reflect with me and together we will seek an encounter with God and his instruments capable of leading us to an experience of miracles and blessings.

It is time that we give each of us the real and conscious opportunity to look at each other through the unfathomable mystery of God's love. It is time for us to remove the darkness, the dullness in our eyes, which are already full of dirt, negativity and evil. It is time to begin to look at each one of us as we really are, facing our real identity and the condition of life in which we find ourselves. It is necessary and time for us to face all dysfunction in our lives and actions. There is a piece of the gospel that I love, where Jesus narrates the healing of a blind man, Jesus touches the man three times, but one of the times the man says: *"I see men as if they were trees" (Mark 8,24)*. I spent a long time trying to make a hermeneutic, which is an interpretation of this verse, and one day, walking through a park full of trees, the Lord made me see their roots, He told me: "It is not the trunk of this tree that makes it firm, nor the beauty of its crown so flowery and full of leaves, but the strength of its roots, the tree takes root". It was shocking for me to have that revelation from the Lord. At that moment I was able to return to the verse I have just narrated to you. The great majority of humanity is rooted, tied, imprisoned, chained, submissive to people, facts, structures, things of the past or of the present, to realities that will only waste our time. How many people rooted to clumsy roots still exist in the bosom of our families? How many people rooted to past mistakes, rooted to negative and hurtful memories of times gone by? How many people rooted to their sins and irregular habits? How many people rooted to loss of persons, status, goods, social condition, etc.?

It is necessary that the Lord rescues our vision, we want to be healed from this blindness which left us for a long time rooted to false possibilities of life. I, in the name of Jesus, by the grace of God, prophesy over you now: *"May your eyes be freed from this blindness, from being trapped, from being chained to what does not allow you to be and to see what God wants to reveal to you. May they be freed from the blindness that does not allow them to see the essence of each one and of what is around them".*

Is it possible that that person who is close to you has no values, that she does not even have even a single virtue of God's grace? Is it possible that she does not have anything positive? Of course not. It is evident that each one of us, in spite of our imperfections and mistakes, bring values and great potential to be discovered and developed by God and ourselves. I invite you to be willing to see, to contemplate, to applaud, to respect and desire to be part of it all.

Essentially I invite you to that wonderful and healing encounter, a liberating encounter where we do not sit in judgment of one another, but to understand that we are God's work. Where we are able to celebrate forgiveness to forgive one another, to seek and offer help, to join forces and expand possibilities for benefits and work.

My greatest desire as Bishop and Pastor of the Catholic Mission of the Divine Nazarene, is that each one of those who come to us with faith, understand this and receive from God the healing of the blindness they bring from outside. My search and work as a servant of God to this wonderful work, is that each one discovers that we are not here just for pleasure, that we are not here because this is the best community, nor because we are the best people, we are here because we have received from God the privilege of sharing together this spring of grace, this spring of blessing, because we have received from the hands of the Lord the benefit of this powerful vision of restoration, of healing, of liberation, of immense restoring love. We are here because we understand that together we must be transmitters and proclaimers of love, that we do not wish to live judging one another or destroying the dreams of our brothers. We are here to go down in faith and humility to the potter's house, as the prophet Jeremiah says: *"...to let the Lord love the clay of our lives, that he may work in us" (Jeremiah 15).* May God's love touch us, may His grace work in us and may the Lord work in us with the strength of His hands, with the efficacy of His love and the power of His infinite mercy. May he work in us the fulfillment of his will. We are here so that the Lord may burn us and test us through the fire of His purification and if there is still something in us that impedes the efficacy of His work, be willing that we may be destroyed and broken as many times as necessary, until the divine potter appreciates in us the work of His hands. At the moment that I am writing this, the Lord gives me a beautiful vision of his purifying fire, of the fire that now burns our souls, of the fire that burns with love. Let us allow ourselves to be purified.

"God of power, God of Justice, God of love, God of majesty, teach Lord the grace of encounter to our souls, open Lord every existing space in our minds, actions, break what needs to be broken, widen our souls, our interior. Lord, enlarge the capacities and the strength of our existence to mark upon us the power of your love and the necessity of our witness to the world".

I know that you, who are reading this book, have a clear perception of where you have failed, how and when misunderstandings rather than encounters have occurred in your own life. I know that you have received from God the necessary light to understand where you have transformed into a fight and battle what could have been resolved with goodness, intelligence and forgiveness, achieving healing and peace.

It doesn't matter if until today you have turned a deaf ear to all that. Therein lies the teaching, no matter if until today you have forgotten the very important and essential meaning revealed when you meet each person in your family. It does not matter if until today you have left aside the possibility of offering and asking for forgiveness. The most important thing now is that you truly open your eyes free of all blindness and allow yourself to embrace, to look yourself in the eyes, to give your hands and to assume the purpose of starting over. I invite you at this moment to think of all the people in whom you wish to reform the bond of love, to bring to your mind those people in whom you really want to have the possibility of an encounter, the possibility of sharing with them an encounter marked by the presence of the Most Holy Trinity. I also invite you to bring to your mind the people of the past who have already died, that you can meet them through the power of prayer in the light of faith, forgive them and receive forgiveness through the grace of God, that you can transform every residue of resentment and pain into a balm of love and joy.

It is time to return to the interior of your own heart, to the interior of your being, to reencounter yourself and seek to make a great evaluation of your life and how you have lived in relation to your commitment to others. Perhaps you are responsible for all the obstacles and hindrances that until today have not allowed the encounters that God wanted you to make. Your blindness was your worst limitation, but now that you have received this healing, give yourself the opportunity, the possibility of reflection, of a deep analysis that will help you understand that you were not born to live alone and isolated, that you are not part of an imaginary world, but that you live in a world inhabited by people and living creatures very close to you. There are people close to you who are ready to offer you all the love and support you need from God.

I see in the masses, in the retreats, in the places where I go, that when people embrace me, they seek through the strong embrace they give me, to find in me something that they lost in some place or opportunity in the past, in some stage of their lives, they seek perhaps the embraces they did not have or that they wish to have, they seek the consolations they did not find in the opportune time. They seek the forgiveness they did not have, the healing of the wounds they are waiting for. I feel that they embrace me with a deep desire to also receive an embrace that will restore their lost dignity. The children, the young, the old, men and women, all are waiting for the grace of restoration. I am, by the grace of God, a fortunate man. I have had the opportunity to make my life a place of multiple encounters. The day I understood the need of my brothers, I said to Jesus: *"Lord, I want to be an instrument of encounters, that your children find you, that they love you Lord, that they do not remain within me. I am willing to go through all confrontations and difficulties, but I want to be a ladder to you Lord, I want to be a springboard by which they jump from their desolations and find peace in your presence. I want to be an instrument of your love, just as St. Francis wanted to be an instrument of peace. I want to be an instrument of their encounter with you Lord. May they see you, hear you and seek you, may they follow you. May they love you, may they receive graces, miracles and blessings from you. And when my last day comes, may I meet you Lord, may you wait for me in your love Lord. May your mercy and justice forgive me of my faults and sins and may you put me in the place of your will, in the place that you have prepared for me Lord".*

Decide to make your life a place of encounter with God, encounter with yourself, encounter with your fellow men.

Every day that passes I realize that time is very short and opportunities are very easily gone. As time passes, sometimes it also drags people and opportunities with it. Don't let your time and opportunities pass you by, especially don't let people pass you by in your life without allowing them to experience God's presence. Give them the testimony of the importance of meeting God, awaken in them and at every opportunity, the desire to search for God. I invite you to offer yourself the opportunity to meet in the miracle of love with each person involved in the mystery of your existence.

This will allow you to rescue the essence of God's love revealed to each one of us.

The encounter will change your life as it changed my life, as it changed the life of the **disciples of Emmaus (Luke 24).** When they met Jesus they felt their hearts burn, they felt all the memories come to their minds and they were able to return to the encounter with the apostolic community. The encounter with Jesus also allows us to return to places that, because of our inconstancy and irresponsibility, we have abandoned. Perhaps you have already left, perhaps you have already separated, perhaps you have already gotten used to the idea that you can live like this, isolated. There is a possibility of taking things back and being able to live healthily in every sense of existence. There is the possibility of a real and definite encounter with Jesus. When this encounter happens, a spectacular power of change will flow within you. This encounter will not remain in itself, but will unfold in a powerful way and other encounters will be born from it. This encounter will give you the desire to return, the desire to share, the desire to tell others of the fire in your heart that makes you burn with faith.

The encounter with Christ will make all your actions exuberant, will transform the beautiful world of your existence into the kingdom of God. When you are able to meet yourself, to meet your fellow men through love and forgiveness, and also to meet God, the Holy Trinity, new realities will open before your eyes. All things will find their real reason for being and existing and the glory of the abundance of the

Almighty God will shine upon you. May God bless you, keep you. Amen. May you make the decision today to begin the possibility of new encounters in your existence, encounters of healing, encounters of liberation and restoration that will make you a new person, restored and blessed, happy and joyful for having given yourself and others the opportunity of a true encounter that will never end. This encounter with God begins here on earth and will lead you to the fullness of eternal life, in the wonderful mansion of God. Receive in your heart, in your soul, the blessing of Almighty God. +Father, Son and Holy Spirit descend upon you, upon your house, your family.

XI. The Light will Lead you to be an All-Inclusive Person

"I am the LORD, in righteousness have I called you;
I will hold you by the hand and watch over you,
and I will make you a covenant for the people,
as a light to the nations". (Isaiah 42:6)

God said: Let there be light. We, as God's creation, are a reflection of his work, we are his image and likeness. Through his love, he himself invites us to show the world the beauty and splendor of the one who created us. We are not just any works, we are bearers of God's light. As Christ himself told us: ***"We are the salt of the earth and the light of the world" (Matthew 5:13),*** we are called to illuminate through our existence, to give flavor and to make love grow and manifest in hearts.

The light reflects the truth, the light fills us with security, the light fills us with peace, because it gives us security of the step towards the way, in it we are never confused. How horrible it is to be in the dark, how ugly when there is no light in our homes, how sad when we look at a city without light. The absence of light limits the power of life. The most beautiful thing is when we can look down from above, from the mountain, especially when we are in an airplane at night and we can see everything, see the lights of the city illuminated, our eyes are filled with grandeur and our heart with emotion. Then, when we are in the countryside or in the forest and there is darkness, we can let ourselves be illuminated by the stars and the moonlight. The light reflected from the celestial lumbars makes us realize the radiance of light, the power of illumination, the strength that exists around us. The light calls us to awaken from the dark and tension-filled nights. It heals us from the sleep of nightmares, from traumas and disturbances. It is the light that frees us from the weariness caused by fear and deprivation, it is the light that can illuminate illness and bring knowledge and grace for healing. It is the light that helps us understand that there is hope and that we can trust in the new that, though we do not see it, is soon on its way. It is the power of light that allows us to contemplate God's mercy and the signs of his work on our behalf, she not only renews, she gives authority. It is the power that directs us on the way. Every good thought comes from the light.

It is the creative beginning, the light penetrates the chaos and makes us capable of separating everything between the good and the evil that exists within each one of us. The greatest effectiveness of the light is its force, capable of making us awaken to a change of consciousness. It helps us to probe our thoughts, it makes us capable of facing ourselves until there are no shadows of doubt in our consciousness, until the shadows of despair, the shadows of fear, are overcome. The light effectively enables us to enjoy the security that comes from God.

How many people come to talk to me in spiritual counseling and ask me, "What can I do to become a strong, secure, solid person?" Full of anguish they tell me: "... things easily slip, they get out of control, I miss opportunities and I don't move forward". The only feasible answer is to teach them and lead them to the protection of the light.

Jesus, in the Gospel, educates us to understand the power of light: *"As long as you have light, believe in the light and be children of the light" (John 12:36).* The light of God is constantly being reflected on the world, the light of God powerfully impels the power of truth on the dark and confused world. Observing the confusion of people and realizing that they really walk as those who are lost among deceptions, lies, bound to their confusions and endless sufferings. I do not remain just observing, immediately what I do is begin the prayer of intercession asking for the power of light to be manifested in them.

"Come, divine light, come, light of God, powerful light that guides humanity from the high heavens, descend powerful light upon humanity that walks under the power of darkness, come upon those who are imprisoned in their miseries, upon those who are lost in darkness. Shine powerfully upon men and women the strength of truth and the desire for transformation, for overcoming, for conversion. Come divine light and dispel all shadows cast by Satan. Come divine light and contemplate the camp of the children of God, their houses, their homes, their works, their challenges. Come divine light and rest upon the men and women of good will, come divine light, inspire in all mankind prayer".

We are a people walking towards progress and improvement, every day we are challenged to overcome huge obstacles and we need enlightenment, intelligence, wisdom. To endure all this requires that we walk under the light of God. It is for this reason that I invite you to awaken what is most endearing in you, to receive strength to come out of the cave of darkness, so that you may begin to enjoy the resplendent brightness of God's glorious light. The great philosopher Plato tells us in the ***Allegory of the Cave***, of the man who lived tied to darkness, tied to the gloom of his imagination for a long time, until subtly, through a crack in the cave, a ray of light begins to enter. This tiny opening was able to conduct the ray of light that led that man chained to the darkness, to be awakened, to start his way, no longer to the darkness, now to the path of light. How many people I know are still like that, still looking against themselves, still unable to see and find the light, still hidden from themselves and from the truth. They believe more in the impossible, in the negative, in cold-ness, than in the strength of life itself. Unfortunately, they are stuck in a darkness of death, their souls are embittered, their actions are totally invalidated because they have closed themselves to the power of the light.

I wish to arouse today in your heart, in your mind, in your capacity to perceive, the desire to return to the light. Come, desire to be released from this dark domina-tion in which you find yourself. Even if you are a little insecure and come walking in the darkness of shadows. Come, come out of the zone of laziness and darkness. Start walking towards the light, even if it costs you, even if it is a little uncomfortable. The light faces the darkness, as the light is unwelcome to our eyes when we wake up. At first, because of its grandeur, it seems to be uncomfortable, but it is obvious, the light comes and frees us from the mask, from the protective curtains that want to keep us in the dark. The light overcomes the zone of confusion, disturbance, lies and self-deception that we develop in our daily life. Light is the bearer of truth that will bring stability by putting everything in its proper place. The light allows us to take possession of everything that has always, in God, been proper to our existence. We were created to be children of light and not children of darkness. We were created to live in the light, in the fullness of the light, to enjoy the eternal light. Christ said: *"I am the light of the world; he who follows me will not walk in darkness, but will have the light of life" (John 8:12).* He who follows Christ does not walk in darkness. We were called to live the strength of the light, the power of the light, the grace of the light, the power of the blessing. What an immensely powerful joy to be told: What an enlightened person, what a person so full of God!

My desire is that your family be enlightened, that your house be enlightened, that your home be enlightened, that your work be enlightened, even if your em-ployers walk in darkness, that you, when you arrive there to work, that they feel the presence of light through you. May your light-filled presence make the world trem-ble through the light that shines through you. Go in and out of places being a light bearer. *"The Lord will keep your going out and your coming in from now on and forevermore." (Psalm 121:8).*

The darkness in the human soul distances it from the power and capabilities possible in God and in this existence. Sometimes we are studying or reading, per-haps lying down, and then we realize that there is a feeling, a perception that can only come from an enlightened idea, from God Himself. That happens very easily to me, when I am at home, resting in my nice space of reflection, but it also happens when I am driving, it even happens sometimes when I am watching a movie. Light is powerful, it has that autonomous authority to penetrate our consciousness and is not limited to anything. Light seeks its place in our being and in our history, it is the force that comes directly from heaven and touches us. No matter the medium, its efficacy is always full and powerful.

The path of light must be sought, longed for perfectly by each one of us if we want to achieve success and blessing. Now I remember that my mother, in difficult times, lived on a ranch and there was no electric light. The light we had was a kerosene light and when the fuel ran out, the light was turned off. Today, she tells me that she thought: "...when my children are born, they are going to live in a house with electric light...", that was my mother's dream, that her children could take advantage of the light, her greatest joy was when she was able to buy the first television, for her it was opening the doors of the world to us.

My purpose is to lead you to understand that we can transform our life, the meaningless life, the gray life, the dark life, into a life and existence illuminated and blessed by the goodness of God. Everything depends on our ability to desire and walk towards the truth. That is, to be able to direct our existence in a way that is centered on the force that is in our mind. The powerful force of light is the power that must be awakened in everyone. As long as you do not enlighten your mind, your whole body will be dark, as long as you do not fill your consciousness with light, your whole being, your whole task, your whole expression will be dark. Light up your mind today with the light that comes from God, light up your mind today with the effective power of the word of God, light up your mind today with the life of Christ, light up your mind today with a good sense of living. Christ must take control of your brain, of your neurons, of your intellectual capacity, of your faculties, of your ethics, of your reasonable conduct, not to manipulate them, but to enlighten them, to orient them towards the good. To advise you to the most good and healthy designs in your life, to make you prosper, grow, overcome and surpass yourself in each new initiative. Make the decision to ask God for the grace to be a being enlightened by the intelligence and wisdom that come down from the high heavens.

An empty mind is an office at Satan's useless disposal. A dark mind can produce nothing but misery, death, disorder, chaos itself, the suffering of oneself, of countless others who suffer the consequences. A dark mind sleeps the sleep of misfortune. That is what we see if we observe that all the time, all around us there are people who literally live in misfortune, people who all the time reveal to be overwhelmed and tormented by Satan. I am a witness of the number of people who look to us saying: "I want to let go, I want to free myself! What do I do?" The answer is simple: Come to the light! Come to Jesus! An exorcism is to break, with God's authority, the forces of darkness over a person's life, to give them the power and ability to take back in faith the power of the grace received in baptism. Exorcism is the victory of light over darkness. Christ, light of the world, Christ of infinite power, capable of removing the darkness from the earth and from our souls. Where He comes, darkness and gloom are destroyed.

If all these misfortunes are trying to take hold of you, it is because you have not yet given yourself the opportunity of a real closeness to the light. Let the light that comes from the will of God descend upon you, the light capable of illuminating everything within you. The light must exist permanently as part of your daily life. It will help you to make decisions, to talk better with the people you love the most, it will be the light that will lead you to get out of where you are and get to where you definitely want to be.

Unfortunately, many times we choose what seems easier to us, unfortunately, we still insist on giving space and seeing things more convenient to the nature of sin. Human nature tends, because of its inheritance of sin, to desire to live in darkness. It is a great illusion of this sin nature to think that darkness is a door to intimacy. This is a grave error and a cause of downfall for many, to live in contempt of the light in order to enjoy a life of passions and vain fleeting illusions. True intimacy is born in the light of the truth in God. The mark of the intimate and secure life is its fullness of light. It is the light of Christ that brings us into total closeness to the truth of all there is. Open your understanding, the main challenge of our lives is to drive out the darkness from within our hearts and move toward the light.

"The night is far spent and the day is at hand; let us therefore lay aside the works of darkness and draw near, that we may put on the armor of light." (Romans 3:12). The decisive moment is at hand for us to exchange the darkness of our hearts for the presence of light. We must seek to fill ourselves with the power of the Holy Spirit. I think that in some ways this decision may seem like a very difficult thing to make, but in reality one thing is linked to the other. If you approach Christ wholeheartedly and you do it fully and decisively, you have fulfilled the fullness of grace in your being. Christ is the light and by drawing near to Him, you also draw near to the light and by drawing near to the light you discover the fullness of truth, straighten your steps in Christ and share the abundance of life.

I am as a priest, bishop and shepherd of the flock of Christ, living the grace of our Lord within my being, within my heart. Obviously it is the Holy Spirit who comes to enlighten and guide me. But it is impossible to pray to the Holy Spirit, it is impossible to claim the power of the Holy Spirit if I step out of communion with the truth, if I do not become obedient to the power of the light. Over the world, darkness is advanced, over humanity and its values darkness is advanced and it is high time that we men and women of good will begin to realize that for too long we have forgotten to realize the need to draw closer to the light. To truly seek the weapons of light. To make real use of the instruments capable of bringing us to the knowledge of the light. *I am convinced that only the presence of the light, the power of the Holy Spirit, the baptism in the Holy Spirit, an inner spiritual renewal of revival in faith, an ardent desire to set out in prayer, can create in us the space for a new life in God from the light, transporting us from non-existence in darkness, to existence now kept in the light of truth.*

How to change this in simple words is an act of decision, it is an exercise of choice, I always say this in my sermons to the quinceañeras: *"Beautiful young lady, you are living the most beautiful age of your life, no one will ever be able to bring back into your life the joys, emotions and capacities of your 15 years of age. Just as it is the most beautiful age, the most beautiful age, it is also the most responsible age, because now you are being presented with the possibilities to make your choices, and everything you choose right will serve your good, however, everything you choose wrong will serve your bad. Many of you will only enter the Church beautifully dressed just now in your 15th year. Many of you will not know how to graduate wisely, many of you will not bring your diplomas, because you will never finish your academic courses, many of you will never enter the church again taken by the arms of your parents to get married, precisely because you will know how to make good choices and many of you will arrive at 40 years old crying, sad because you did not do what you should have done. Make the most of it, Miss, your opportunity is now... give your heart to life, fill your heart with light and hope, follow Christ and make your life a reflection of God's goodness".*

Light calls us to commitment, light calls us to truth. It provides us to recognize that good things always cost efforts and a lot of perseverance. Everything that is in the light costs human act, divine act, attitude of faith and responsibility. It needs decision and desire to remain worthily faithful to the end. The things that are obtained in an easy way have their origin in the darkness of the darkness, they are in the deception. Normally deception wants to trap you, wants to lead you on the easy and clueless path, and then throw you directly into the abyss of misfortune. However, the light enables us to overcome every obstacle, even if they are hard and difficult, the barriers often seem insurmountable, but for those who choose the light of truth, they will never be impossible to overcome. Every challenge overcome in the light of the Lord enables us to enjoy the blessing of the light, in the light and by the light.

"I stand at the door and am knocking, whoever hears my voice and opens the door will receive my presence, and I will come in and dine with him." (Revelation 3:20).

In the midst of the dark night of your existence, Jesus is knocking at the door, in the dark night of your fears, of your failures, in the dark night of your darkness of sins, Jesus is knocking at the door, because He brings the light. He is the light. And Jesus is saying to you: Let me come in, I want you to understand me and begin to walk in the light, to live in the light.

It is a great grace, but it is also an immense benefit when we assume our total surrender to Jesus Christ. *It is a time of conversion, of change of route, of beginning a new dialogue, a time to be a person in fullness by the grace of God. Time of change of perspectives, time of maturity, of salvation of the youth, of the family, of the society. Time to sow new ways of living and living together. Time to begin to love responsibly.*

What hurts me most is to see young people plunged in darkness and the agnostic authority acting strongly to expand the darkness, the lack of faith. To see in young people the darkness of the denial of God, the denial of the virtues of the spiritual life. All this is happening because there was a lack of light in the homes, because there was a lack of light in the parents, because there was a lack of light in the social system. Someone has to be a prophet and begin to say that in these hearts there is light, and that the light is Christ, we have to raise with the strong voice of love, to announce the generosity of God that awaits them. It is time to prophesy with faith and prayer so that they have the opportunity to return from these catacombs of darkness to find the holy place, glorious and blessed, the very heart of Jesus. I do not know how is your house, your home, your family, your closest ones, but you can prophesy today the time of the coming of the light. Today you can prophesy that your home will be transformed into a room illuminated by the grace of God. The true and real effort for salvation is to open yourself to the light. Attention, everything that is in front of you needs light. It allows us to see things with the real clarity of their concept. If you enter an unknown place and this place is in darkness, it will take you a long time and the help of other senses to understand and move between each thing that is in that place, trying to know how to understand its meaning.

However, if you arrive at an unknown place and there is light in this place, everything that is there becomes easy for you to interpret, because light has that power, light takes us out of ignorance, takes us out of disturbance and permeates us directly into the womb of the truth of every being that exists.

Light is the powerful force capable of enlightening our mind and awakening the deepest feelings of our heart, not towards submission, but towards obedience through the truth, that is why Jesus told us: *"You will know the truth and the truth will set you free" (John 8:32).* It is the same as saying you will know the light and the light will set you free. No one knowing the light will remain bound, the future, tomorrow is always around us, but in the morning we need the light, what we will live in the future will not remain chaotic, but it will be illuminated by the power of the light, this is a real evidence in the life of many. Life is in real chaos because of the absence of the power of light. Jesus said: *"No one lights a lamp to hide it or to put it under a drawer. On the contrary, it is placed in a high place so that it may give light to all who enter the house. A person's eyes are like a lamp that illuminates his body. Therefore, if you look with sincere and kind eyes, light will enter your life, but if your eyes are envious and proud, you will live in complete darkness. So be careful, do not let the light of your life go out". (Luke 11:33-35).*

This life, whether it is short or whether it is long and lasting, for I do not know how many more years God will allow me to live. I plan to live for many years, but I do not know for how long. I am like a candle in the midst of people, I want to be consumed by the light of God and to illuminate until the last day of my existence every heart, every person, every mind, every home, with the light of Christ and of my vocation. This illuminated candle of love will continue burning, I do not know until when, this wax will burn and this body will give itself each day to the service of the Gospel. I want to consume myself enlightening my brothers, I want to give my existence without ceasing to be an incandescent spark of God's love and this will ensure that my future will be from here, a heaven on earth.

I invite you to desire and seek to be a perennial light, a constant light, no matter the size of the wick and the spark, what is necessary is that you are not a firefly that lights up, goes out. Stay kindled. Be constant in the midst of great difficulties. The problem with fireflies is that now it shines and then it flickers and this is not the mission of the church. We are the body of Christ, called to illuminate the world, as living and vibrant torches, witnesses of the light, which has to maintain its condition of light for the people.

Many young people come to me saying: I want to be a doctor, I want to be a teacher, I want to be an engineer, a mechanic, a nurse, a dancer, others want to be just rich, all of them I bless, because of my love for them I get excited to hear their desires and to see the struggle that some of them have already started. I also see the young people here in the church, those who are finishing their careers, or those who are just starting, those who still have a few years to go, but are already looking beyond, to them I carry them in my prayers and I always bless them and I prophesy over them declaring in them the power of God's light, so that they remain strong and never falter in their path. To all I remind them not to turn away from the light of Christ. Everything that you are going to live tomorrow depends on the light that is on from today, you can do absolutely nothing if you refuse the light.

A few months ago I received one of these guys from the church who came to visit me, he was here in Long Beach on vacation and he told me that he came home and almost every day he was here, he cried. His parents brought him to talk to me. They asked me, "We want to know why our son is crying so much. I looked at them with a lot of love, but told them absolutely nothing. As soon as I spoke to the young man, with whom I had always had a lot of affection and closeness because I had known him since he was a teenager, I looked at him and asked him: *"Do you realize now what light is? After spending so much time in darkness, now you have seen the light again. From now on, wherever you are, wherever you go, you have to carry the light. The light that shines on you is the light that comes from the high heavens, the light that you received at your baptism, the light that has confirmed in you the faith through the sacrament of confirmation and the shining light of Christ's presence through the sacrament of the eucharist. Now it is your mission to keep that light and to make your existence and the existence of all those around you shine."* The boy cried for a few more days until he understood that the light of God exists, and it is God himself who shines and illuminates, who scorches and burns within each one of us. To see the light, to live the light and to share that mystery is a work of great responsibility.

May all share in your life, in your victories, and may all see your faith and the strength of your enlightenment and know how to say: "God, work of your hands, God first! Who is like God, no one else but God! Happy is he who has believed and blessed, who has rested in this truth! Embrace the light and enlighten your own existence by the power of God's word, seek the effective understanding of God's word, through the life of faith and the life of prayer. May it be so. God bless you always.

"I praise and bless you O almighty God, I want to draw near to you Lord, in a very particular way, to rest in you all my trust, my hopes and desires, to acknowledge the authentic power of your infinite mercy and declare that I truly recognize that you are in immediate control of all things, you are the one who reigns, who rules, you are the one who disposes every single thing, however challenging and testing it may be, it will always for us be signs of blessing. Teach me, Lord, to understand your words, teach me, Lord, to understand your divine will and lead me, Lord, along the path of intimacy with you. May every moment be an opportunity to contemplate the greatness and honor of your glory. You Lord, remain the goal, you remain our rest in spite of all the questions and doubts along

the way, of all the worries, of all the fears, you remain the refuge where we can rest, in whom we can place all our longing. Lord, blessed are you, we enter your most holy presence leaving our hearts in your divine presence so that you can take charge, so that you can fill them with your love and your peace. I want to lay my mind at your feet Lord. To prostrate all my thoughts in your presence. Only you can enlighten me, give me the discernment I need, only you can lead me as your beloved child and make me pass where I need to pass, mighty God, merciful God, God of goodness; renew over me your word and your power, strengthen all my being, organize all my living. I consecrate to you all that I am, I give into your blessed hands and await your holy will. I consecrate to you all my brothers and sisters so that you may help them to understand the greatness of your love and teach them to live the glorious experience of your love, bless them, keep them. Give them the powerful force of your infinite kindness so that they may also enjoy your ineffable mercy, your love and your divine compassion. All this I ask through the power of the Blood of Christ today forever and ever. Amen.

Biography

*Monsignor Rodrigo Romano Pereira, Brazilian, son of Antonio Pereira (in memoriam) and Selma Romano. Bishop of the Holy Catholic Apostolic Brazilian Church. Philosopher and Theologian by the Saint Sierge Orthodox Institute (Paris), postgraduate in Psychopedagogy by the Saint Joseph University (Beirut). Preacher of retreats of Inner Healing. Exorcist with great spiritual authority. Teacher of Biblical Schools and Urban Pastoral Courses. Bishop of the Diocese of Long Beach, CA. since 2013 and Primate of the Church in the U.S.A. Man of faith, bearer of authentic principles of deep spirituality, excellent pastor of souls and promoter of disciples in the faith. He has dedicated all his knowledge, academic tools, tradition and education in the Holy Doctrine to the service of the people of God and charity to those in need. His greatest goal has been to offer the word of God and the power of the sacraments to those who have strayed farthest from the truth. A lover of prayer, he has exercised his priestly ministry teaching thousands of people the spiritual path of intimacy with God. He entered the seminary at the age of 15 and has been searching for God for more than thirty years. He has had many pastoral experiences in different countries and cultures. Brazil, his homeland, Colombia, where he strongly experienced his call and devotion to God. Dominican Republic, where he founded a community of sons and daughters of the Divine Mercy. France, where he took his academic classes and was able to develop in the Charismatic Renewal groups the gifts and various charisms offered by the Lord. In Lebanon he faced the painful experience of the conflicts of the war being a witness of obedience and fidelity to God and the people. In the United States, ten years after announcing the Gospel through the Catholic Mission of the Divine Nazarene, a charismatic-apostolic community of faith, founded by him in the company of some very important faithful for the foundation of this work of God: **Irma Gallegos, Engelbert and Araseli Rodas, Juan Rubalcaba and Araseli, Gloria Estivias, Martha Velazco, Leticia Melgoza, Hayde Endter, Nancy Granados, Maria Diaz and Diac. Raul Peña.** With God's grace he has been a faithful worker and worthy servant of the word for the work of God.*

Dedications

To the people of God, to all men and women of good will, who have given me the opportunity to live the fullness of service to God through humanity.

To my mother Selma, to my father Antonio (in memoriam), who with their love and struggle did their best in love to instill in me a great person. To my mother for being my companion of all hours and first missionary of the Divine Nazarene in Long Beach, CA.

To my brothers Diac. José Mauro, Mauro Antonio, Marcio Andrey, who have left me the legacy of the example of sobriety and honesty.

To André, Sister Magdalena, who have been instruments of God's love and true support of loyalty and faith in all my commitments in the different fields of work.
To my godparents Daniel and Juanita, Felix and Rosario, who have supported me and kept me in the most difficult moments to maintain my ministry and the work of God here in this mission.

To my godchildren Eduardo, Fernando, Vianney, Brisa, Rigoberto, José Manuel, Anthony, Isabela, Alberto, Gastón, Esmeralda, Sergio, Sonia, Félix, Sandra, Steve, Linda, Jesús, my closest children to whom God has allowed me to bring blessing and love, to those who have desired to follow my teachings with faith and discipline of life.

To Ana Maria, who has been in the mission and during this work an exemplary secretary and spiritual daughter, always offering the best of herself.
To His Excellency Most Reverend Dom Josivaldo Pereira de Oliveira, Presiding Bishop and President of the Episcopal Council of ICAB, who always brings me peace and testimony of life, who every morning speaks to me and inspires me to be salt of the earth and light of the world. You will forever be my Spiritual Father in the Episcopal ministry.

To the Holy Catholic Apostolic Brazilian Church, to the Holy Council, to the Sacred College of Bishops, to the deacons and priests who give their lives with so much commitment and testimony of love.

Thank you!

+Rodrigo Romano

Made in the USA
Columbia, SC
28 June 2021